Strike Free

Strike Free

New Industrial Relations in Britain

Philip Bassett

MACMILLAN
LONDON

First published 1986 by
MACMILLAN LONDON LIMITED
4 Little Essex Street London WC2R 3LF
and Basingstoke

Associated companies in Auckland, Delhi, Dublin, Gaborone, Hamburg, Harare, Hong Kong, Johannesburg, Kuala Lumpur, Lagos, Manzini, Melbourne, Mexico City, Nairobi, New York, Singapore and Tokyo

British Library Cataloguing in Publication Data

Bassett, Philip
Strike free : new industrial relations in Britain.
1. Industrial relations—Great Britain
I. Title
331′.0941 HD8391

ISBN 0-333-41800-X
ISBN 0-333-41801-8 Pbk

Typeset by Rowland Phototypesetting Limited
Bury St Edmunds, Suffolk

Printed in Great Britain by
Anchor Brendon Limited, Tiptree

Contents

Acknowledgements

Industrial relations are constantly in flux. Any attempt to fix at a particular point their complex, shifting pattern runs the risk both of being arbitrary and of being superseded by the unravelling of events. Nevertheless, the developments *Strike Free* tries to describe seem to me to be important strands in the pattern.

Many people have been of great help to me in the preparation of this book. That includes virtually everybody named in it (all quotations are from interviews with the author unless otherwise indicated), and many more besides. I would like to thank all of them, and the many employees, employers, trade unions and their officials, managers and their companies, civil servants, journalists and academics who gave generously of their time, and in doing so helped shape my thinking and the book itself – though the responsibility for it remains mine.

In particular, I would like to thank Nick Chapman and Jim Reynolds for their assistance in writing the book itself; my colleagues at the *Financial Times*, especially the labour staff, for their help and forbearance. Special thanks are due to John Lloyd, for his guidance, example and friendship, and, most of all, to Elizabeth and James – for making it worthwhile.

Abbreviations

Acas Advisory, Conciliation and Arbitration Service
ACTT Association of Cinematograph, Television and Allied Technicians
Apex Association of Professional, Executive, Clerical and Computer Staff
ASTMS Association of Scientific, Technical and Managerial Staffs
AEU, AUEW Amalgamated Engineering Union
CAC Central Arbitration Committee
CBI Confederation of British Industry
CP Communist Party
CPSA Civil and Public Services Association
DE Department of Employment
EEF Engineering Employers' Federation
EESA Electrical and Engineering Staff Association (section of EETPU)
EETPU Electrical, Electronic, Telecommunication and Plumbing Union
EMA Engineers' and Managers' Association
GCHQ Government Communications Headquarters
GMBATU, GMBU, GMWU General, Municipal, Boilermakers and Allied Trades Union
IBM International Business Machines
IDS Incomes Data Services
IMS Institute of Manpower Studies
IoD Institute of Directors
Jetro Japanese External Trade Organisation
MSC Manpower Services Commission
MORI Market and Opinion Research International

Nalgo National and Local Government Officers' Association
NEDC National Economic Development Council
NGA National Graphical Association
Nupe National Union of Public Employees
NUM National Union of Mineworkers
NUR National Union of Railwaymen
PAT Professional Association of Teachers
Sogat '82 Society of Graphical and Allied Trades
Tass Technical, Administrative and Supervisory Section (of the old AUEW)
TGWU Transport and General Workers' Union
TSSA Transport and Salaried Staffs' Association
TUC Trades Union Congress
Ucatt Union of Construction, Allied Trades and Technicians

1

'Unthinkable Pacts'

'You ain't seen nothin' yet!' Ronald Reagan's words, climaxing every speech of his successful 1984 US presidential campaign, were at once a challenge, a promise, and – to his opponents – a threat. When Eric Hammond, general secretary of the electricians' union EETPU, growled them at a baying TUC Congress in the fading gilt splendour of Blackpool's Opera House in September 1985, the implications were much the same. Hammond dominated the TUC that year, dogged by reporters, bathed in television arc light. Twelve months earlier, the figure holding centre-stage had been Arthur Scargill. In 1985, the miners' president sat alone in a Blackpool tea-bar; in 1984, he had cupped the TUC in his hand, with only Hammond and one or two others holding out against the emotion of the miners' titanic strike, warning that fine words at the TUC would melt away on the picket lines. Then, they had howled Hammond down: 'Hitler would have been proud of you lot,' he snarled, after the TUC's aggressively euphoric delegates had forced him to brief silence.

What the rapture for Scargill and the vitriol for Hammond demonstrated, though, was more than just a rhetorical division in the heady atmosphere of a conference hall. The two men, in some ways markedly alike – both intelligent, both tacticians, both rabble-rousers, both fervent, both careful – stood for political, social and industrial attitudes that were wholly incompatible: for the one, a revolutionary challenge through militant vanguardism, explicitly rejecting the considerations of market economics for his industry, and resting his deliberate affront to the established order entirely on the most stark of class perceptions; for the other, an equally explicit rejection of class-based industrial enmity in favour of mutually beneficial co-operation, pragmatically embracing social and technological change, resting his market-based vanguardism on the aggregated assent of the individual. At the 1984 TUC Congress, this unbridgeable gulf remained a hidden agenda, while the sound and fury of the miners' strike raged on the surface, appearing only when Roy Sanderson, the EETPU's national engineering officer, attempted to defend the strike-free deals he had negotiated; like Hammond, he was all but howled from the rostrum. A year later, it was all in the open: the miners were defeated (largely at their own hands, fatally exposed by those trade union members who had refused them support), and the EETPU was riding high, though everywhere under attack: for signing no-strike agreements, for reaching single-union deals, for refusing to back the NUM, for applying for Government money to fund its postal ballots. But the EETPU came through Blackpool unscathed; it was the TUC which emerged embarrassed, foolish, unnerved.

'New realism' – a pragmatic reassessment of the unions' role in the light of Labour's appalling 1983 General Election defeat – had been born in the same town two years earlier. It was dealt two heavy blows by the banning of unions at GCHQ and by the miners' strike, but the dominance of the EETPU and its ally, the AUEW, at the 1985 TUC Congress saw it publicly born again. It is the electricians who embody this new form of trade unionism, and the strike-free deals which it and other unions have signed with a small but growing number of companies are its most obvious practical manifestation. Tom Sawyer, Nupe's analytical deputy general secretary, is clear about the connection: 'No-strike deals are part of the new realism which encompasses a more slick professional non-party-political trade unionism. If these deals continue then trade unions become meaningless as workers' organisations – they become part of the management.' Ken Gill, general secretary of Tass, agrees: 'The difference between a slave and a worker is the right to withdraw his labour. So while the pendulum arbitration agreement does not specifically forbid strikes, it obliges both sides to accept the arbitrator's verdict, thereby denying the workers the ultimate expression of rejection.'[1] Sawyer's general secretary, Rodney Bickerstaffe, goes further: 'What such organisations are saying is "We will be less militant, we will be more accommodating, we will crawl lower and further, if you will give us membership." In the same way as a scab says "I will accept even lower wages, if you give me the job." It is the denial of collectivism, it is the denial of the basic trade union concept of, so far as is possible, fair dealing.'[2]

Hammond's and the EETPU's argument is that collectivism has been denied, not by the EETPU, but by those it is supposed to include – working people. They point to the TUC's coverage among employees – now down to well below 50 per cent. They point to the sharp declines in union membership in the recession of the early 1980s. They point to the especially high incidence of non-unionism in what are seen as the two potential employment growth areas of the economy, high technology and the service industries. They point to the collapse of old industries in areas traditionally strong in trade unionism, and to the establishment of the new in areas where trade unionism is far from the norm. They point to demographic changes in the workforce, and in its attitudes, its support, its ambitions.

They do not see strikes as part of that pattern. Nor do others: David Warburton, now second-in-command at GMBATU, describes as a 'shortsighted and obsolete view' the attitude that strikes are employees' only effective weapon against their employers. 'The right to strike', says Hammond, 'has been put aside, not abolished.' The strike is in any case a dangerous weapon to wield, capable of causing – indeed likely to do so, the EETPU suggests – self-inflicted damage as much as hurting the opponent. The strike-free deals negotiated by the electricians and others – at companies like Toshiba, Sanyo, NEK, Inmos, Shopco, AB Electronics, Sharp, Irlandus, AVX, Hitachi, Xidex, Shotton Paper and Nissan – offer a balance, providing for single unionism, single-status, full work flexibility, a measure of industrial democracy, arbitration and no strikes: each of those has benefits for both employer and employee.

Strikes in the UK fell in 1985 to their lowest number for fifty years. Most employees don't go on strike; MORI found at the end of 1985 that only a fifth ever had. When they do, it is never a clear-cut business, but a tangled complex of often conflicting reasons and emotions. Striking is far from a simple matter, and it is not something done lightly. Many British employees do not or cannot go on strike – 330,000 in the armed forces, 140,000 police, 247,000 nurses, 37,000 members of the Professional Association of Teachers, 13,000 ambulance staff, and probably 9000 covered by the range of strike-free agreements – about three-quarters of a million. The Conservative Government would like to see more: its 1983 election manifesto promised action on limiting strike action in essential services like water, gas and electricity.

Labour has no declared objection to strike-free deals; all it states is that they should be entered into voluntarily. The agreements reached by the electricians and others are exactly that, and employees covered by them are positively enthusiastic about their effects. As society, employment and trade unionism continue to evolve, there will be more to come. 'Unthinkable pacts,' Hammond forecast at the TUC. 'You ain't seen nothin' yet.'

2

Strikes: The British Disease

Sunday night in April in north Nottinghamshire, wet and cold. It is eight weeks into what will become, what clearly is already, the most serious and significant strike in Britain since the 1926 General Strike. Britain's miners have been on strike since the National Coal Board unexpectedly announced the closure of a pit called Cortonwood, and made clear it was seeking cuts in overall coal capacity of 4 million tonnes per year. That is to say, most of the miners are on strike; in Nottinghamshire, the picture is different. There, after early confusion about the area NUM's stance, a ballot of members in the county has produced a clear result: the Notts men are going to work. They have been heavily picketed, especially by miners from across the county border in Yorkshire. There has been considerable violence, including the first death of the strike – though worse is to follow.

Publicly, Arthur Scargill has barely acknowledged the widening gap opening between Notts miners and those on strike over the NUM leadership's decision not to ballot the union's membership on national strike action, though such a ballot is required by the union's hallowed rule-book. The lack of a ballot was to run like a sore through the strike, and its contagion eventually to kill it; the Nottinghamshire gap was eventually to become a gulf into which the NUM itself would all but completely collapse. Now, though, Scargill's stance will do no longer: tonight, in the small town of Kirkby-in-Ashfield, he is to open a short and fruitless campaign to persuade the Nottinghamshire miners to join the strike. The venue is a hall above the town's modern, purpose-built shopping centre. The brick square at its heart is crowded with miners, their wives, their families. When the doors are opened, there is a rush up the stairs, as if it is a football match, to get the best seats. It seems clear that the entire audience is actively supporting the strike: at the opening of his campaign to convert those Notts miners who will not join it, Scargill is to speak to the already converted. Inside the hall, as the early speakers get into their stride, the atmosphere is tense, expectant: for many, this will be their first physical glimpse of a man, crucial to their lives, whom they have seen before only on television. 'Is he here?' go the whispers. Rumours of his arrival ripple through the packed hall. Necks crane to be the first to spot him.

Quietly, Scargill slips in through a side entrance. As he enters the room, the audience bursts into a standing ovation, drowning the voice of the current speaker. Settled, the miners wait. As Scargill rises to speak, the audience joins him, wildly applauding. His speech is a towering performance. Its message to those not on strike is an odd one, of beseeching dismissal, but to those in the hall it is everything they could have wished for: passionate, powerful, scathing, funny, densely packed, vivid, committed, strong – theirs. The standing ovation at its conclusion outdoes with ease the previous two.

Scargill over, most of the reporters at the side of the room rush off: telephones to find, deadlines to meet. In doing that, they deliver the words of Scargill's speech, but they miss its real impact. When the speeches are over, a curious phenomenon begins to shape itself in the hall. The miners – the men – leave. The women, and the children, stay, and begin to form up in a long queue round the walls of the room. Predetermined or not, it is hard to tell; certainly Scargill sits on at the top table, as ever unruffled. The women line up in front of Scargill – to kiss him, and to hold their children up to be kissed. 'Do you know who that was?' asks one mother of her child, as she leads him away from his kiss. The child shakes his head. His mother leans down. 'When you're a grandfather,' she says, 'you'll be able to tell your grandchildren that you were kissed by Arthur Scargill.'

In the 1984–5 miners' strike, that kind of loyalty to Scargill, bordering on devotion, was hard for those living in the south, including Government ministers, to comprehend, but it was crucial to an understanding of why the strike started, why it went on so long, why it mattered. It had its corollary, too: as much as Scargill and the strike inspired that kind of near-reverential commitment, it generated the opposite. Among the working miners, Scargill was a hate figure, maniacal and oppressive. The miners' strike, as a stoppage, was both untypical and an absolute: the first because

Scargill's fervently political perceptions turned it into a revolutionary challenge, a level of intensity to which few strikes aspire; the second because, in its image, its violence, its passion, its effect and its sheer length, it took to the limit all the strands of Britain's strike pattern which had come to be called the 'British disease'.

'Most trade unionists have never been on strike,' according to the TUC.[1] 'Workers rarely need to use the strike weapon to compel employers to bargain with them,' the TUC went on. 'When strikes do occur, they do not only hurt the business and the community the business serves, they hurt the workers involved.'

In the cold light of the mid-1980s, that looks almost obvious. By the end of the 1970s, there was little sign of that kind of cool, self-appraising awareness. Britain had been hit less badly by strikes in the years of Labour's social contract with the unions, years during which the unions effectively took on the role of policing their own members. But the pressures were building up. Crucially, the 1977 biennial conference of the TGWU rejected Jack Jones' impassioned pleas, and voted for a policy of free collective bargaining. Although it seems barely credible now in the mid-1980s that a policy decision at a trade union conference could have that kind of impact, once the TGWU had made that decision, the Labour Government was living on borrowed time. Its ill-judged attempt to wrest another year of pay restraint from the unions, and Prime Minister James Callaghan's arrogant attempt to tease the delegates to the 1978 TUC Congress in Brighton by toying with the date of the General Election, paved the way for the rash of strikes which took place that winter. By its end, almost 20 per cent of the British workforce had been on strike, from oil-tanker drivers to hospital porters, from lorry drivers to journalists, from train crews to gravediggers. Though the number of strikes in 1978 and 1979 actually fell, the amount of days lost through stoppages soared to more than 29 million – the highest since 1926, the year of the General Strike (see Figure 2.1).[2] Reaching, unusually, for their Shakespeare, the newspapers dubbed it the 'winter of discontent'; that it would make glorious summer for the Conservatives seemed inevitable. For Labour, its claim to a special relationship with the unions smashed, electoral disaster looked a foregone conclusion.

Charging itself with the complete reshaping of the unions, as a central part of what was to be little less than a cultural remodelling of Britain, the new Conservative Government set about its task with relish. Cleverly, too: no longer was it to be the big-bang approach of

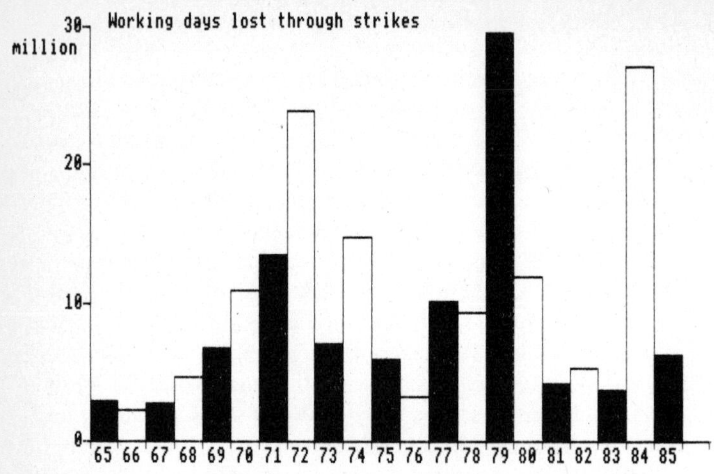

Figure 2.1: UK strikes 1965-85 Source: DE

ten years before, adopted by both Labour and the Tories. This time, it was planning, it was strategy, it was stealth – and it worked. Most importantly, it worked in its widest sense, in the grandest of its ambitions. By focusing the thrust of its underlying arguments on the undeniable arrogance of some union leaders ('When a Labour Government disagrees with the trade union movement,' Ken Gill, Tass general secretary, told the 1978 TUC Congress immediately after Callaghan had spoken, 'then it is almost certain that the Government is wrong')[3] and on the gap that had opened up between those leaders and their members, the Conservatives struck at the heart of the unions' *raison d'être*: representativeness. The effect was to change the way workers thought about unions, thought about themselves. By 1985, virtually everyone bar the hardest of the hard left, for instance, accepted that ballots before strikes and for the election of union executives – the core of the Conservatives' most far-reaching piece of labour legislation, the 1984 Trade Union Act – were a fixed part of industrial relations' legal framework, not to be swept away by any incoming government. Attitudes were altered by the Conservative onslaught, and nothing – the TUC, the Labour Party, the unions themselves – was left untouched by it. The dog would no longer allow itself to be wagged by the tail.

But the new Conservative approach worked in the short term too: the number of strikes, of those taking part in them, and of working days lost by them, plummeted. This decline in strike activity was not readily apparent, because in every year so far of Mrs Thatcher's Government there has been a major public sector strike: steel-workers in 1980, civil servants in 1981, health workers in 1982, water workers in 1983, the miners in 1984 and 1985, the teachers in 1985 and 1986. But removing from the figures the days lost through what the Department of Employment lists as major disputes shows a virtually static pattern. Stripping out the number of stoppages in the coal industry from the DE's statistics paints a similar picture.

At least, it shows that the Government's strategy worked for a while. The start of the miners' strike in March 1984 sent the overall strike figures soaring once more: in 1984 the number of days lost through strikes, leaving aside major disputes, and the number of non-coal stoppages was the highest since the winter of discontent. Research by the Institute of Manpower Studies[4] seemed to confirm that, at bottom, little had changed. In about half the twenty-five organisations examined in the IMS study of strike activity in 1984 the level of action had fallen in the period 1982–4, but, significantly, most of the employers concerned did not see that fall as a signal change in industrial relations. Instead, it was regarded merely as a response to recession, a temporary staging-post. Some of the organ-isations in the IMS survey were gloomily predicting a resurgence of industrial action if and when job prospects improved.

Maybe so; but by 1985 the pattern was shifting again. 'Britain is enjoying its most strike-free year for nearly fifty years,' said Kenneth Clarke, Employment Minister, at the end of 1985. Clearly, the strike figures gave cause for such quiet jubilation: the number of stoppages in the year almost halved 1984's figure; the total number of disputes recorded by the Department of Employment was the lowest since 1936. The reasons may be numerous: the failure of the miners' strike led many employees to doubt whether taking action themselves could be successful; there has, too, been a clear shift away from strikes towards other forms of industrial sanctions. But for the Government, it was the law, and in particular the pre-strike ballot provisions of the 1984 Act, which yielded the most convincing explanation. However, the pay research company, Incomes Data Services (IDS) suggested that ballots were not the cause of this sharp reduction in action[5] and there was some justification for this view: ballots monitored by Acas in the course of its normal duties showed, firstly, that while there were certainly more ballots than previously, their number was still small, covering only a minority of disputes. Most strikes are not pre-planned strategies, but flare-ups, in the main not even making it into the Employment Department's record of strikes; indeed the DE's figures show that most recorded strikes last for three days or less. Even where there were ballots, in the more prominent disputes, the votes were going in favour of strike action, by about 2–1. So the Government's explanation is not wholly tenable.

But what the bald figures fail to include is the change in attitude engendered by the 1984 Act's provision. Faced with well-known examples such as the London Underground workers' refusal to heed an unballoted strike call by the NUR in 1985, or the rejection of action by guards in the same union even after a ballot and on an issue – trains without guards – on which they had public sympathy, anecdotal evidence clearly suggests that the prospect of balloting (and obviously of losing) has restrained moves towards action that even in straitened times might otherwise have gone unchallenged. Survey evidence supports that view. Polling by the industrial communications company EPIC showed that in January 1984, when the provisions of the 1984 Act were widely known though not yet in force, 75 per cent of trade unionists thought that ballots before strike action would make very little difference to the outcome of industrial disputes; by October, with the Act just taking effect, the figure had barely changed – 73 per cent.[6] But by May 1985 the drop was much more marked – 62 per cent. Of course, there is still a majority who are sceptical about the impact of ballots (perhaps because they are aware of the real form and duration of most strikes), but the number is falling – and is likely to continue to do so.

So if the number of strikes is falling, is their importance declining too? 'It is unfortunately beyond doubt', said a major Department of Employment report on strikes issued towards the end of the strike-hit 1970s, 'that Britain has a poor industrial relations image and probably true that the whole community suffers from it.'[7] Strong stuff in such a formal survey; it went on to suggest that strikes affected trade and Britain's competitive position. It is demonstrable that strikes do affect the economy directly, in terms of lost production: the 1984–5 coal strike, as an extreme instance, caused losses of approximately £180 million to British Steel, £323 million to British Rail and £2 billion to the Central Electricity Generating Board, as well as £1.75 billion to the National Coal Board itself. But the overall effect of the more usual run of strikes is probably considerably less than absenteeism, for example. 'Since 1977', says Maurice Phelps, board member for personnel at British Shipbuilders, 'we've actually lost about half a per cent of working hours in industrial action – and of that about one-tenth I suppose would have been official.' But he says: 'If we could reduce our absenteeism by one per cent, we would be much better served.'

Absenteeism in some companies is high. At Vauxhall, for example, absenteeism was running at up to 22 per cent in 1985 at its Ellesmere Port and Luton plants, according to union figures. Research compiled by the Industrial Society suggests that it is in the service sector, source of many of the new jobs, where most UK absenteeism lies, rather than in the old, heavy (so-called 'smokestack') industries. And all absenteeism rates are many times greater than the strike figures for their particular sectors.

That absenteeism causes industry more problems than strikes, in terms of productive time lost, is clear; that strikes cause more damage overall, often for wholly different reasons – connected with a company's image, its reputation for reliability or otherwise, for good or poor management, for a co-operative or difficult workforce – is clearer still. 'For a number of years,' the DE study said,[8] 'our industrial-relations image has tended to create the impression abroad that British industry is "riddled" with strikes. This is reinforced by frequent use in the foreign press of "the English sickness" to refer to the deleterious effect of bad industrial relations or "the British disease" to refer to labour disputes.' Shooting the messenger is always easier than swallowing the message; while world reporting of British industrial relations may not have been all that UK governments desired, the central problem was not with the journalism but with the strikes. Virtually every study ever carried out on international strike comparisons (notoriously difficult to compare though they are) reaches the same conclusion about the UK's strike performance: broadly middle-ranking in terms of direct contrasts with other countries' strike figures. Figure 2.2 illustrates this. As far as it goes, that is true enough. But the 'middle-ranking' conclusion does tend to obscure two key points. First, the view of Britain as strike-prone is rooted in the *nature* of British industrial conflict, where strikes have apparently been seen as an inevitable step in an industrial dispute, rather than as a weapon of last resort. Compare Italy, which, although at the top of the international strike league table, is in an important sense less plagued by the effects of strikes.

Again, this is because of the nature of strikes: Italian stoppages tend to involve large numbers of workers, often for little more than one day, and are often political in motive – industry itself is less affected. Secondly, the spread of the countries included in the international statistics obscures the fact that among its principal industrial competitors – notably West Germany, France and Japan – Britain's strike record is worse, and noticeably so.

In part, though, Britain's international strike standing may not matter overmuch, especially in the wake of the rejection of militancy as an industrial tactic which the failure of the miners' strike implied. One test of that – and worries about the UK's international strike record are constituted in precisely these terms – is inward investment. Japanese manufacturers, for instance, are among those most determined to maintain production, and so are among those most anxious to avoid strikes. Research carried out by Professor John Dunning at the University of Reading shows that, although Japanese companies see British industrial relations as a negative factor, it is only one of a whole range of factors to be taken into account: some are more attractive – lack of EEC tariff barriers in particular – but others are considerably less so – component supply, availability and

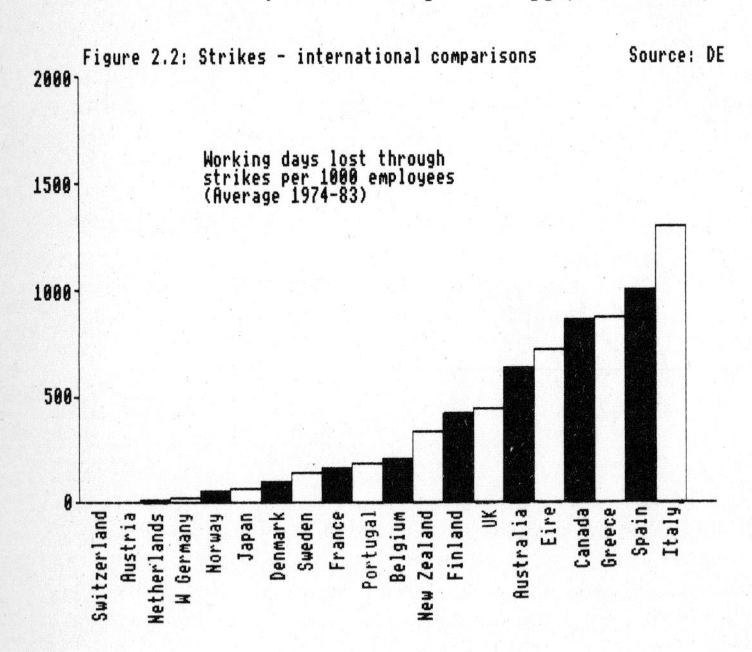

price, for example.[9] If improvements can be made to the pattern of British industrial relations in practice, the image once presented of the UK as gripped by the British disease becomes irrelevant. A combination of event and design has achieved precisely that.

3

The New World of Work

Strikes during the winter of discontent made a vital contribution to the Conservative victory in the 1979 General Election, and reforming the trade unions was placed at the centre of the Government's whole ideological, economic and social strategy. But this was not an isolated policy: it both drew from and contributed to decisive and perhaps permanent changes not just in industrial relations, but in the economy, in industry, in employment more generally. All these changes are inextricably interwoven. Even so, some elements were more crucial than others in developing a new world of work, their impact more keenly felt and likely to have the greater implications for the future.

Work and the Law

When the Conservative Government came to power, unemployment in the UK stood at just over 1.3 million, or 5.6 per cent of the working population.[1] The jobless total had been rising before then, of course – markedly so in 1971–2 and 1974–6. But by the end of 1985 it stood at almost 3.2 million, or 13.2 per cent (see Figure 3.1), though the Labour Party, the TUC and other organisations, taking into account the numerous changes in the method of compiling the official unemployment statistics and the 675,000 on special job-creation programmes, put the 'real' unemployment figure much higher, at 4 million plus. Within the overall increase as measured by the official statistics, there were clearly discernible characteristics: increases in unemployment among adult men, among young people, among those out of work for a lengthy period. By the beginning of 1986, the Government was still claiming that the trend

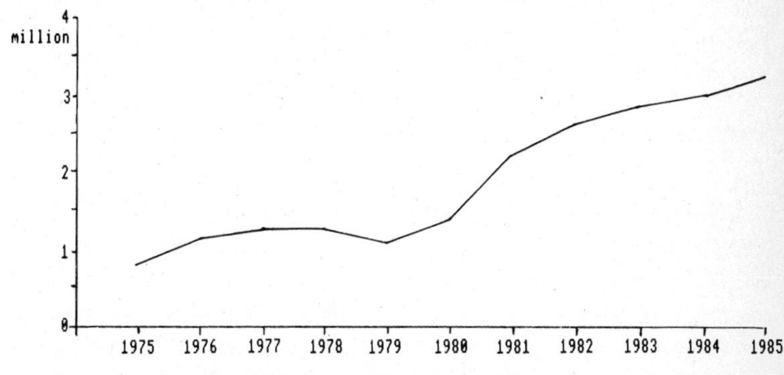

Figure 3.1: UK unemployment at June each year 1975-85 (seasonally adjusted) **Source: DE**

in unemployment was broadly flat. Although inflation seemed to be under control, the claim tacitly accepted that there seemed to be little prospect of unemployment falling, at least in the reasonably short term.

Unemployment, according to poll evidence, is now considered to be the foremost of the UK's problems. That perception arises partly out of a genuine moral concern; but it is prompted, too, by a real fear of being out of work. In October 1985, MORI found that 85 per cent of those surveyed had not been unemployed in the previous two years; a majority believed that they would not be out of work in the same period in the future. But a substantial proportion – 37 per cent – believed that it was very or quite likely that they or someone in their family *would* be unemployed in the near future. That fear of unemployment, just as much as the reality of it, has been crucial in helping to determine the new world of work. Estimates of the likely path of unemployment differ widely, often varying according to the political complexion of the forecasting organisation. Few are free from this bias, but Bain predicts a roughly steady or marginally increasing rate of unemployment to the end of the decade.[2] If that prediction, or something like it, is correct, it suggests that some of the industrial relations shifts – in both attitude and practice – seen in the recession are likely to continue.

But as unemployment has been rising, so has the pattern of employment been changing. In the five-year period to 1985, the number of employees in employment fell by more than 1.6 million, or just over 7 per cent. That movement contains a number of important trends. The fall in the numbers employed has been almost entirely among men. Male employment in 1980 stood at just over 13 million, or nearly 60 per cent of the total. By 1985, this figure had fallen to just over 11.5 million, a decrease of almost 1.5 million jobs – more than 11 per cent.

In contrast, female employment fell in the same period by just over 300,000. However, within these figures there are again important trends: since mid-1983, male employment has continued to fall (by 164,000, to mid-1985) while female employment has risen (by 413,000). The increase is almost solely in part-time working. In overall terms, part-time female employment in mid-1985 was, at 46 per cent, little changed from its position five years before, when it stood at 42 per cent; but the change is enough to account for almost all the increase in female jobs, and for 95 per cent of the increase in employees in employment.

The pattern of self-employment has also changed. From 1975 to 1979 there was a small but steady decline in self-employment, and from 1980 to 1983 a steady increase. But from mid-1983 onwards, the numbers rose sharply, by almost 400,000 to a total of 2.6 million.

Part of the explanation is sectoral. As manufacturing was hit, so jobs were lost: 1.4 million in the five years to 1985, a fall of more than 20 per cent. Most of the reductions have been in jobs held by full-time male employees: in 1975, for instance, 5.2 million men were employed in manufacturing – ten years later, the figure had fallen to 3.8 million. Offsetting the decline has been a shift to employment in the service industries – 1 million over ten years, half of it in the two years to mid-1985. Much of that service employment is part-time and female, though self-employment is also high in services, at 62 per cent. Bain forecasts that all these trends are likely to continue.[3] The TUC suggests that much of the 'apparent' recovery in employment since mid-1983 can be accounted for by the increase in people holding two jobs: in 1979, there were an estimated 370,000 'double jobbing', while by 1984 this had grown to about 700,000.[4]

Occupationally, too, employment structure has been changing.

The Engineering Industry Training Board, for instance, charts significant reductions in categories of engineering employment in the ten years to 1984: operators down by 31 per cent, craftsmen by 21 per cent, technicians by 15 per cent, supervisors by 31 per cent. But scientists and technologists showed an employment increase in the industry of more than 40 per cent over the same period, reflecting the increasing technological mix of the workforce.[5] Employers have tried to come to terms with these changes, and have perhaps accelerated them, by trying to use their labour more efficiently, more flexibly – using more temporary workers, for example. Temporary employment grew by 11 per cent in the two years from mid-1983. According to an IMS survey, 68 per cent of companies surveyed now employ temporary workers, with 55 per cent of those increasing their use of such workers since 1980.[6] Overall, then, though the workforce has grown in the five years to 1985, it has done so only in certain areas: among women, among part-timers, among the self-employed.

Politically, Labour has seen in this the development of the two-tier labour market: 'An elite of highly skilled technical and professional workers, and the mass of the less skilled, contract workers and homeworkers, hired and fired at will with few rights or benefits.'[7] The Government has seen it as a vindication of its economic and industrial policies. It has intervened directly and repeatedly in the labour market. This has been effected in part by the schemes and initiatives put forward by the Manpower Services Commission, whose role and funding have greatly expanded with the increasing emphasis on training. Government intervention in the labour market has taken another form, too: the series of moves against trade unions, which the Government has seen as an undesirable labour-market rigidity preventing the creation and the expansion of employment.

The steps taken against the unions have been varied. Not least important has been the attempt at attitudinal change, trying to stimulate a scaling down of the importance of unions in people's lives. In this the Government has achieved some of its greatest successes – helped in good part by the unions themselves. But it is legislation which has been most significant. Chastened by the failure of the previous Conservative administration to reform the unions in one all-embracing move, the 1979 Conservative administration boxed clever. Its succession of measures – the 1980 Employment Act, its 1982 namesake and the Trade Union Act 1984 – were cumulative, hedging in the unions with measures concerning secondary industrial action, for instance; or votes before strikes; or internal electoral practices (some of which – especially those of the TGWU – did not stand the test of public scrutiny); or the provision of public funds for unions' own internal ballots.

Changes in unemployment, in employment, in Government thinking and in employment law, all played their part in creating the new world of work – but they were far from being the only factors.

New Areas of Work

Industrially, Britain has for long been seen, and has seen itself, as two countries, crudely divided: heavy industry in the north, the Midlands, Scotland and Wales; agriculture and lighter, clerical and service industries in the south. It is broadly true that there is indeed such a division, though there are obvious exceptions – coal mining in Kent, for instance, or lush farming in part of Yorkshire. Steel, coal, shipbuilding provided the jobs of industrial Britain; offices, electronics, hotels were jobs for the soft south. Those were the stereotypes. But when the labour shake-out started in the recession, the stereotypes held true. Table 3.1 shows the location of redundancies since the Conservatives came to power in 1979.[8] Least hit are those areas where employment is in any case lower – East Anglia, the south-west. Despite the stereotypes, London and the south-east are hit, and hit hard, but from a high employment base. Worst hit are the old industrial areas of Merseyside in the north-west, Yorkshire, Birmingham and the black country in the West Midlands. Redundancies in the north-west alone over the period were half as high again as those in the West Midlands. Taking just two heavy industries – steel and motor manufacture – the roll-call seemed endless: 7000 jobs gone at Ravenscraig; 8000 at Linwood; 5000 at Consett; 3000 at Hartlepool. At Scunthorpe, 8000; 10,000 in Sheffield; 6000 in Liverpool; 9000 in Shotton. At Bilston, 3000; at Corby, 8000; at East Moors, 7000; at Port Talbot, 8000. The list goes on.

'Where are the new jobs?' was the plaintive question put throughout 1985 by the tripartite, consensual National Economic Development Council.[9] Where they weren't was in the old industrial heartland areas (see Table 3.1).[10] Where were they? With the exception of Scotland, where multinational high-technology companies committed considerable capital investment in new plants, they were

Table 3.1: *Redundancies and vacancies under the Conservative Administrations since 1979*

	Redundancies	*Vacancies*
South-east	170,995	288,100
Greater London	219,404	144,300
East Anglia	35,504	30,100
South-west	133,444	75,100
West Midlands	261,156	59,500
East Midlands	164,387	47,400
Yorkshire and Humberside	252,884	52,300
North-west	373,039	79,600
North	184,753	41,000
Wales	145,376	42,000
Scotland	260,641	92,200

Source: DE

in the industrial cradle of the new industries – in London (primarily services) and, most of all, throughout the south-east. Many were rooted, too, in computer-based technologies. The provision of regional grants in development areas like Telford or Milton Keynes attracted some new companies, but a considerable number clustered in three areas, each consciously modelling itself on California's 'Silicon Valley', in which are gathered a great many highly productive semiconductor-based companies. One of these areas is the M4 corridor, running west from London to South Wales. Loosely based in its eastern part on the Thames Valley, so winning for itself the title of 'Britain's Silicon Valley', some definitions stretched it to include towns like Basingstoke or even the Southampton area, where satellite companies sprang up around IBM's sites. Another is Scotland's central lowlands – 'Silicon Glen' – and the third is the area encompassing Cambridge and its immediate environs – 'Silicon Fen'.

There, in Silicon Fen, one study shows a remarkable growth of high-tech companies to a total of 322 in the area – 72 per cent of them starting up in the six years to 1984.[11] Keeble and Kelly, surveying computer electronics companies in the area, found more than 11,000 employed across 136 plants, with an average size of eighty-one employees – roughly 22 per cent of them skilled workers, compared with 17.8 per cent semi- and unskilled in all computer companies, and as few as 7.5 per cent in newly established companies.[12]

The effect on local labour markets of such shifts in employment patterns can be dramatic. Impressionistic views of Liverpool, on Merseyside, and of Newbury, at the heart of the M4 corridor in Berkshire, support the notion of a divided Britain: in the one, cheap clothes in the shops – in 1985, jackets for 45p – in what was once the city's most prosperous shopping street, and mile after mile of physical devastation; in the other, shopping-centre car parks filled to overflowing every day, property prices soaring, a local antique auction taking £0.25 million in a single day, and rashes of new, single-storey computer companies squeezing in wherever they can. Harder evidence of job growth in the area bears this out. Newbury stands in the centre of the M4 corridor, whose Government research establishments attract small high-tech firms around them, and generate more entrepreneurially minded scientists with a grasp of the potential commercial application of some of the work. The M4 corridor is important, too, in the assembly and distribution of American high-tech products.[13] All of this probably feeds back into Ministry of Defence work, which absorbs on its own about a third of the electronics industry's output, and so maintains the cycle. Berkshire County Council estimated in 1981 that 12 per cent of all new companies were high-tech, compared with 4 per cent of established companies; 57 per cent of the high-tech companies surveyed were not even in existence five years earlier. Employment in high-tech firms had grown by 10 per cent over the previous five years, with high-tech jobs accounting for 12 per cent of all private-sector employment, or about 20,000 jobs in all.[14]

In the computer industry, Keeble and Kelly find that only 8.8 per cent of new employment is in the conurbations, while 31.9 per cent, by far the largest figure, is in small towns.[15] More widely, research work carried out by Newcastle University's centre for urban and regional development studies presents detailed evidence on Britain's divide.[16] Champion and Green constructed an index based on five variables for individual local labour markets: unemployment rate (for May 1985, the survey date); employment change 1971–8, and again 1978–81; population change 1971–81; and households with two or more cars in 1981. Using this index, they could measure with pinpoint accuracy the local economic performance of individual towns. Precisely because they bear out so clearly what were previously only felt beliefs, the results are significant. Table 3.2 shows Britain's ten best towns, and the ten worst.

The towns performing best, such as Winchester (population change 1971–81, + 3.88 per cent; employment change 1971–8, + 49.16 per cent, 1978–81, + 7 per cent; unemployment rate, 4.1 per cent of the total working population; households with two or more cars, 24.14 per cent), are seen by the CURDS researchers as 'the most promising geographical basis for Britain's future economic development and long-term prosperity'. Winchester itself is a microcosm of industrial change: a strong local employment financial sector, with more than 20 per cent of its population classed as employers, professionals or managers (half as much again as the national figure) and four-fifths of its jobs in the service sector (compared with two-thirds nationally). The best performers – 'boom towns', the

Table 3.2: *Britain's best and worst towns (local economic performance)*

Best	*Index*	*Worst*	*Index*
1 Winchester	0.764	1 Consett	0.137
2 Horsham	0.726	2 Mexborough	0.154
3 Bracknell	0.719	3 South Shields	0.155
4 Milton Keynes	0.702	4 Coatbridge and Airdrie	0.159
5 Maidenhead	0.697	5 Hartlepool	0.182
6 Basingstoke	0.697	6 Sunderland	0.184
7 High Wycombe	0.693	7 Bathgate	0.215
8 Aldershot and Farnborough	0.690	8 Liverpool	0.217
9 Bishops Stortford	0.677	9 Irvine	0.228
10 Aylesbury	0.675	10 Birkenhead and Wallasey	0.238

survey calls them – form an arc around the western half of the London region, from Aylesbury and Milton Keynes in the north to Crawley and Haywards Heath in the south. The next eighteen highest-scoring local-labour-market areas complete the ring – though, significantly, London itself is not included. Only then oil-rich Aberdeen – placed nineteenth in the Champion–Green index – breaks the pattern of south-eastern dominance.

The worst towns are more scattered, in the north-east, South Yorkshire, Tyne and Wear, Strathclyde, South Wales and Merseyside. The majority of the worst-performing areas are the cities; the best, the research concludes, are 'relatively small towns which are situated in essentially rural areas'.

Such local economic success was reciprocal: created by new enterprises, it attracted more. There were other reasons, too – among them improved communications (close to motorway networks), a better living and working environment (no more smokestack industrial skylines; instead, science and technology parks, purpose-built industrial estates), and even fashion (for a computer company in the early 1980s, a Cambridge address was in itself a virtual passport to business, trailing in on the coattails of the then untarnished reputation of Sir Clive Sinclair). Crucial, though, was the supply of labour. Labour was obviously available in other parts of the country – probably more so. But what the new companies wanted was a new labour force, with new characteristics: young, compliant, eager, with no history of militancy, and untouched by any culture of trade unionism.

That the boom areas of the south could provide exactly that combination is clear from the geographic dispersal of trade union strengths. Geographically, union organisation had simply reflected the geography of industry, and had developed traditions of organisation stemming from that – GMBATU in the north-west, for instance, around major employers like Pilkington, the St Helens-based glass manufacturer, or the AUEW in the West Midlands, the home of the engineering industry. But as the pattern of industry changed, as the older industries declined and the newer ones, providing far fewer jobs, sprang up in their wake (sometimes literally: Telford's industrial estate, for instance, bursting with computer-based companies, is built on the site of an old, closed coal mine), the unions failed to modify their own geographical organisation: the engineering union has nine district offices in the West Midlands, an area in decline, and only one to cover the entire, expanding area of Basingstoke, Farnborough, Andover and Guildford.[17] Instead, their patterns of organisation were altered for them, by industrial change: they lost more members in those areas where industries were in decline. Take the engineering union. According to a study by Massey and Miles,[18] in the immediate post-war years half the union's membership was in five areas: London, Lancashire, Birmingham–Coventry, South Wales and Glasgow–Paisley. In 1951, the union had 3500 more members in these areas than in the rest of the country combined. By 1979, even before the present recession began, these areas had 120,000 fewer members than in what had once been the union's periphery. After growth in the non-heartland areas came a less sharp decline as the recession bit: the study shows that in the two years after 1979, overall AUEW membership fell by 17 per cent – but the decline in its heartland areas was steeper still, at 22 per cent.

Organisationally, then, unions have been slow to respond to membership changes thrust upon them, but employers have not been slow to relocate. A number of factors have helped determine companies' location: grants, transport, similar companies in the same area, labour-market issues such as the growing requirement for unskilled, often female, certainly cheaper labour. But unionisation levels have been a vital element. Research suggests that some of the areas with the lowest levels of unionisation, such as East Anglia and the south-west, are rated by companies – particularly in the new, electronics industries – as having the most co-operative and the best-quality labour forces.[19]

A good example is Scotland, which began to attract foreign-owned plants in the 1950s and 1960s, but where almost a third of American-owned plants (especially those in the high-technology industries) have opened within the last ten years. The outcrop of plants is phenomenal. From the USA, IBM and National Semiconductor at Greenock, Motorola at East Kilbride, Digital Equipment at Ayr, Burroughs Machines and Sperry Univac at Livingston, General Instrument at Glenrothes and Hewlett Packard at South Queensferry. From Japan, NEC at Motherwell, Terasaki in Glasgow, Nippon Electric at Livingston and Mitsubishi at Haddington. From West Germany, Klockner-Moeller and Siemens at Cumbernauld, and WSK at Glenrothes. From the Netherlands, Philips and MEL at Dunfermline, and Arcotronics at Bathgate.

In an effort to win further investment, the Scottish Development Agency in 1984 surveyed the US-owned manufacturing plants based in Scotland.[20] The results, covering 133 plants (78 per cent of the total) and comprising 83 per cent of manufacturing employment, paint an impressive picture: high-quality labour (90 per cent of managers interviewed at the US plants thought it so), high levels of flexibility of working (88 per cent of plants – 95 per cent of high-tech plants – saw it as good or very good), increasing productivity (87 per cent of all plants) and good investment prospects (58 per cent – 75 per cent in high-tech companies).

Just as impressive was the industrial relations picture: the SDA found most of the plants surveyed to be dispute-free, with four out of five having experienced no stoppages at all due to industrial action since 1979. Even when stoppages did occur, their impact was negligible; in the seven plants which experienced stoppages in 1983, for instance, the total number of working days lost as a result of them was 0.09 per cent. A majority – a narrow one – *did* recognise trade unions – 56 per cent across the whole survey, though this level fell sharply in the high-technology companies. For those with unions, though, the results were good – 92 per cent considered unions in their plants to have a favourable or neutral impact on plant operations; compared to a similar survey two years previously, the proportion of favourable to neutral was shifting towards the former. Whether they had unions or not, most plants surveyed enjoyed a remarkable stability in industrial relations: in the vast majority of cases, their labour agreements provided for arbitration as the final stage in negotiation – and almost 86 per cent said that their workforces always (50.4 per cent) or usually (35.3 per cent) followed such procedures through. Labour turnover is very low – 1.5 per cent at Levi Strauss, for instance, or 4 per cent at Digital Equipment – and there is a Japanese-style commitment to the company: 'Often,' a Hewlett-Packard manager told the SDA survey team, 'people want their whole family to work for Hewlett Packard.' A Motorola manager agreed: 'Our staff are interested in Motorola; they take a lot of pride in the company. A lot of people would never want to leave the firm.'

Sometimes, though, the picture can look a little less rosy. In spring 1985, National Semiconductor at Greenock announced that 450 jobs would have to be lost at the plant, where a year earlier further investment of £100m had been welcomed by the Government. But even as the redundancies were being proclaimed, some of the workforce – young (the company's average age at the time was seventeen and a half) and predominantly female – were testifying not only that they had never thought of joining a union for some chance of protection against precisely such developments, but that even when it had happened, they still had no intention of doing so.[21]

So it is clear that it is not just the managements of companies in these areas who do not want trade unionism – their employees are not much keener.[22] Some unions have made special efforts in the new areas of employment. The EETPU, for instance, decided to base for the first time ever a full-time official in Milton Keynes. Both the electricians and the white-collar union ASTMS have organised recruitment drives, including leafleting, hotel meetings and such official and unofficial contacts as are possible, in the M4 corridor, where they think there may be a potential market of up to 30,000 new members. Their appeal to employees in these areas is frank: 'You are ambitious and not afraid to admit it. You are prepared to change your employer at critical periods during your career. The M4 professional is confident and optimistic – but life is not without its difficulties.'[23]

Tass, originally a purely white-collar union in the engineering industry, has become more widely based, through mergers with smaller craft unions and through the technological blurring of distinctions between crafts. It has targeted one Berkshire town, Bracknell (third on the CURDS index) for a special campaign, including a mailshot to every house in the town, to draw in new members: 'Bracknell and its surrounding districts, more than any other area in the south-east, depends on high technology industries,' it said in recruitment literature,[24] combining a concentration on place with a general analysis of skill shortages and of the union's efforts to counter them. But such efforts by the unions have had little success; and they are coming up against as much resistance from employees as from employers. Two reasons for that need to be examined: high-technology work itself, which together with the people it attracts seems to be notably resistant to trade unionism; and the changing nature of the workforce, especially in these industries and in these areas – different ambitions, different hopes, different perspectives.

Work and High Technology

High-technology, computer-based companies are now consistently cited as one of Britain's few growth areas in the economy, one of the few possible sources for new work, new wealth. So-called 'new' technology is now widespread in British industry. In 1978–9, the TUC agonised for months about what stand to take towards the new technologies, whether to accept them or oppose them. But the ground moved too quickly: a 1985 Policy Studies Institute survey found that plants covering 73.8 per cent of manufacturing employment used microelectronics technology either in the products they made or in the production processes with which they made them.[25] Predictions of large-scale job losses[26] were mostly unfounded: the PSI found that in 1981–5, an average of 74 per cent of UK manufacturing establishments saw no change, or even an increase, in jobs due to the use of microelectronics technology.

Mostly, too, employees embraced technological change positively, often finding in many cases that it helped and enhanced their work. Batstone *et al.* found in their shopfloor survey that employees across a whole range of industries and occupations were either neutral or often favourably disposed towards technical change; those against it were either very few or, in some cases studied (chemical and food and drink plant maintenance), there was no opposition at all.[27] The PSI study found similar results: of the disadvantages found by manufacturers in using microelectronic technology, only 7 per cent rated union or shopfloor opposition an important factor (much lower than in Germany, or France), and much less of a problem than skill shortages or development costs.[28]

Survey evidence also shows that the use of high technology runs hand in hand with growth.[29] Anecdotal evidence bears this out: at a Telford high-tech company in summer 1985, growth was vividly apparent – internal walls being knocked down, trucks driving straight into the planned production areas to unload new equipment, a palpable sense of energy and excitement among the small workforce.

But concurrent with growth runs instability; linked with the sheer pace of technological change and fierce competitive pressures, the result for many of the UK's high-tech companies was volatility, astonishing levels of performance, interest and profit generating over-confidence, overreaching – and then disarray. Bruised and battered, drawing in their horns, some (like Acorn), at least survived; many (like Sinclair) did not. In 1985 came an astonishing about-turn in the fortunes of the electronics industry. Share prices of even some of the leading companies like GEC, Plessey, Racal and STC lost half or more of their value. With an oversupplied market, strong international competition, and changes in traditional customers – the Ministry of Defence, for instance, becoming increasingly cost-conscious, and the privatisation of British Telecom leading to indications that it might be looking elsewhere for suppliers – even the larger companies felt a chill. 'High-tech' as a label once meant an inbuilt financial advantage as far as potential backers were concerned; it was not long before it was being equated with high risk.

Inevitably, that change hit some areas harder than others – and the blows were all the more difficult to bear because the promise had been so great. In Swindon, for instance, which has shed its old, railway-dominated image and replaced it with another based heavily on the new technologies, high-tech started to hurt: by autumn 1985, there had been 180 redundancies at the US electronics company Square D and 110 at Logica VTS business computers; Intel, the semiconductor manufacturer, froze all recruitment and sent its staff on an extra week's unpaid holiday; National Semi embarked on a cost-cutting exercise; Kode International, the computer group, announced redundancies at its Kam Circuits and Kode Services plants; and Plessey announced that its signal technology factory in the town would be shut after only a year's work, and operations shifted elsewhere.[30]

Probably, though, such patterns are little more than microcosms of the overall trend of the recession; the belief that high-tech would shield whole areas from its impact proved to be unfounded. But as in the economy generally, for those who stayed in work the rewards were good. A survey by the Engineering Council in October 1985 showed that the earnings of technician engineers had risen in real terms by 15.5 per cent since 1979, compared with a 9.6 per cent average increase in earnings, after inflation, in the same period.[31] The pay research company, Incomes Data Services, reported in August 1985 that high-tech pay was roughly stable, despite the industry's problems, with no sign of the virtually instant pay-cuts of 10 per cent or more seen in the USA, though in some areas the rate of pay rises had fallen to 7–9 per cent – still well ahead of inflation.[32]

So, even in such turbulent times, pay in the industry held steady. Job satisfaction is high, too. In Unimation, a robotics manufacturer in Telford new town, one line-worker enthused about his job, but even his keenness could not match that of his wife: a secretary in the company, she came in on Saturdays and her days off to learn about the robots, in order eventually to work with them. But the work is individualistic. Production lines tend to emphasise collectivism.

Much supposedly high-tech work, such as television manufacture, is still like this – but much is not. Much of the work demands individual effort, individual concentration. Focusing solely on a VDU screen cuts employees off from each other, exaggerates individualism. Imaginative skill and flair in carrying out such work, in bringing it to a successful conclusion, excludes others; pay systems geared to rewarding such individual achievement reinforce it.

Hardly surprising, then, that the level of trade unionism is low. The Engineering Council survey found that unionisation among technician engineers in the private sector is only 31.9 per cent.[33] Among Scottish US companies, the slim majority recognising trade unions is far from reflected in high-tech areas: although non-unionism is a feature in 44 per cent of all US-owned plants there, in electronics plants the non-union level is 63 per cent, in high-tech oil-related plants it is 73 per cent and in similar health-care plants it is 86 per cent.[34] Scotland is far from being the most prominent case in its high-tech opposition to trade unionism. The Electronics Location File survey of 905 companies in the electronics industry (roughly a quarter of the whole industry, at the time of the survey) shows that a fraction under 60 per cent of all electronics companies do not welcome union membership among their employees,[35] and where it is not welcomed, it tends not to exist (see Figure 3.2). Even where unions have managed to get a foothold, in practice it may not be much more than that: 59 per cent of the unionised companies, for instance, do not encourage union participation in decision-making, though most do not regard unions as harmful – 88 per cent see them as positive or neutral forces within the company, least co-operative on pay and redundancies, and most helpful in recruitment and in the introduction of new working methods and new technologies. Low levels of unionisation seem to go hand in hand with good industrial relations: 77 per cent of companies rate their own industrial relations as good, and while company loyalty may be distorting these figures, in general 89 per cent see industrial relations within electronics as a whole as fair or good.

That industrial relations stability is reflected in the low level of industrial action (see Figure 3.3). In only 5 per cent of all companies surveyed was there a strike; most of the industrial action involved action short of striking, such as overtime bans or working to rule. Action was more pronounced in the East Midlands and the north-east, and least so in the south-west and the west.

Unions trying to organise in the high-tech sector have tended to

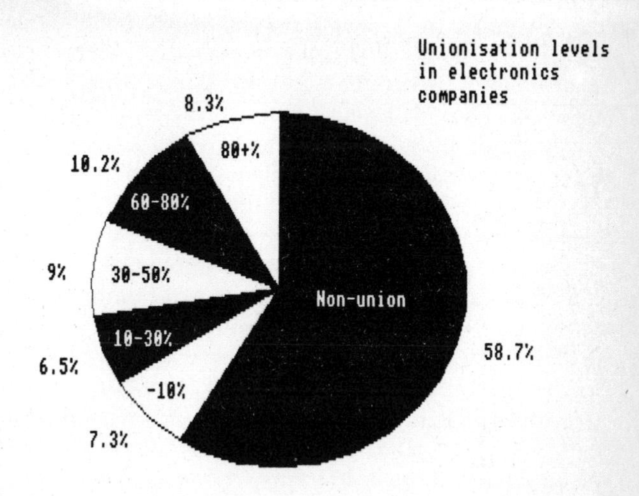

Figure 3.2: High-tech unionisation Source: Elec.Loc.

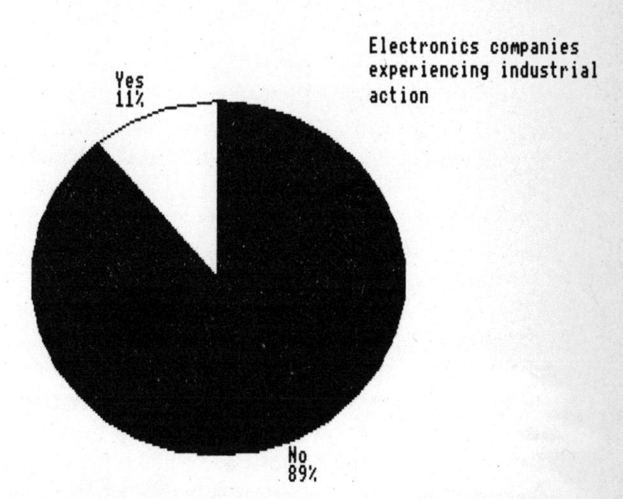

Figure 3.3: Strikes in high-tech Source: Elec.Loc.

emphasise their constructive, practical approach. Tass, for instance, has tried to focus on specific problems, such as skill shortages and training needs, in an effort to make a professional appeal to employees used to making judgements on exactly that basis. Tim Webb, ASTMS electronics officer, stresses the connection between new technology and trade unionists working with it: 'To large numbers of trade unionists, there is nothing "new" about new technology. Professionally qualified trade union members in the large electronics companies have researched, developed and applied the technology. *They are* the new technologists.'[36]

Webb stresses, too, the importance of training and of procedure agreements concerning the introduction and operation of new technology (though research suggests that these have been actively pursued by only a small number of white-collar unions, and their spread and content has been much less than was originally hoped for by the TUC).[37] But he also includes the possibility of industrial action, in new, high-tech forms:

> The employer will be pressurised by new electronic dispute methods as well as the traditional withdrawal of labour and the picket line. . . . the tactics adopted will need to be far more sophisticated and planned well in advance, rather than a mere withdrawal of labour by a particular group of, say, computer operators.[38]

Webb was writing in the wake of well-publicised industrial action in the Post Office and Civil Service; his predictions now look more speculative. Privately, union officials with members in such areas testify to the small likelihood of such action in the current climate, at least partly because of the effects of the computer labour market – the Government, for instance, has had to reach special pay deals for its computer staff in an only partially successful attempt to prevent them from selling their skills elsewhere in what is at present a seller's market.

But in an important sense, given the trade union penetration levels in high-technology areas, these are hardly the relevant questions. What currently confounds the unions is how to organise employees in these areas, how to persuade them not of their industrial muscle, or otherwise, but of the advantages of trade union membership. 'Every union thinks that they have found a way of dealing with it, but we haven't,' John Tuchfeld, a Tass national officer, told a conference on unions' recruiting in high-tech – probably the first of its kind – organised by the Technology Policy Unit at Aston University in Birmingham in late 1985.

Tuchfeld gave as an example the growth of software houses. 'We are finding it immensely difficult to organise software personnel,' he said. 'They are at the present time in considerable demand. They can set their own price.' Tass in particular needs to organise in this area. Its core as a union is draughtsmen, but with the widespread move away from drawing-boards to computer-aided design on screens, much of its members' traditional work has shifted away from in-house employees to software houses – effectively contracted out. 'Software companies pay high wages,' says Tuchfeld. 'Their employees don't see the need for a union. And we aren't at the moment making any headway at all with persuading them about the moral position' – the idea of joining trade unions for the greater good. That inclines towards socialism; and it is apparent that in many areas of the working class, and especially among the new technicians of the high-tech companies and in areas of the country where such industries are now increasingly to be found, the moral force of socialism no longer strikes a responsive chord.

The New Employees: Reconstruction in the Working Class

'Socialism is not inherent in the consciousness of the working class, but is one possible development among others. Socialism has no privileged pathway to the heart of the working class; on the contrary, it has to fight every inch of the way.'[39] Blackwell and Seabrook's careful charting of the constant change in the British working class – 'constantly being augmented, and constantly being left behind'[40] – its fluidity, its suggestibility, its malleability, is a startling and convincing analysis. It stresses the working class's continual refashioning of itself, its tangled complexity, its diversity, its refusal to be encapsulated as homogeneous. Among its insights is the perception that the idea that the working class is a natural supporter of the Labour Party was probably obsolete even in 1945, at the return of the Attlee Government, which may prove to have been the apotheosis of working-class political power. Blackwell and Seabrook's emphasis on anecdote, parable, myth and common experience as being of central importance in comprehending the working class precludes the simplicities of analysis of electoral voting patterns; crude, partial attempts to sum up a complex structure of feeling. True enough; but at the same time voting shifts do give a picture, however limited, which is in one important respect central, because such shifts are the raw data on which political parties operate. Moreover, as every union leader publicly conceded after the 1983 General Election (and it was a perception to which they began privately to give primary operational significance), Labour had to win the following election if either the unions or the Party were to stand any real chance of survival as credible representative social forces.

The 1983 election was a disaster for Labour, as Table 3.3 shows. Its share of the vote was its lowest for sixty years, since the 1922 election at which it had polled 29.7 per cent.[41] For Labour, the obvious, though no less damaging, effect of the 1983 election was to shatter its hopes of regaining power – not, for many Labour leaders, realistically high during an election campaign which saw Labour both divided and on the defensive, the Conservatives riding hard the British victory in the Falklands war, and the Alliance fragmenting the opposition vote. But within the overall sense of disaster for the Party were some chilling insights. According to a confidential analysis prepared four weeks later by Larry Whitty, now Labour's general secretary but then secretary to the unions' main electoral machine, Trade Unions for a Labour Victory: 'Trade union support for Labour fell by 4 per cent in 1979 and a further 12 per cent to 1983. No other separately analysed group shows so sharp a decline.'[42] Figure 3.4, based on private polling evidence carried out for Labour by MORI, shows the decline in Labour voting among trade union members, and its eclipse by the total non-Labour trade union vote. Behind the General Election votes lies a complex pattern. Whitty's

Table 3.3: *The 1983 General Election result*

	Votes	%	*Seats*
Conservative	13,012,316	42.4	397
Labour	8,456,934	27.6	209
SDP/Liberal	7,780,949	25.4	23

Source: F. Craig, *Britain Votes 3: British Parliamentary Election Results 1983* (Chichester, 1984)

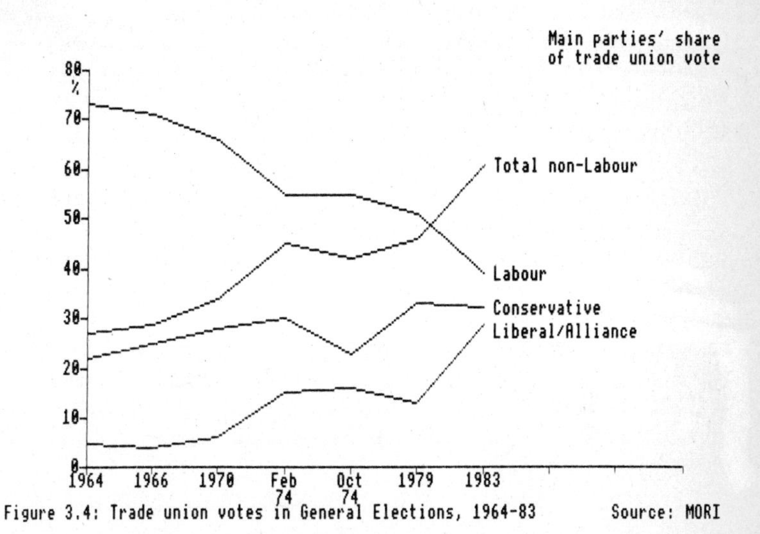

Figure 3.4: Trade union votes in General Elections, 1964-83 Source: MORI

private paper showed Labour's union vote slumping to as low as 33 per cent at the end of 1981, with the Alliance peaking then among trade unionists at 51 per cent. After the Falklands, much of that vote had switched back to the Conservatives, with 32 per cent of the union vote, signalled by intention, and Labour recovering to 36 per cent. At the beginning of the 1983 election, Labour's potential union vote of 49 per cent was virtually back to its May 1979 election figure. But by the end of the election campaign, that vote had slumped by 10 per cent – all of that 'massive' loss, according to Whitty, had switched to the Alliance.

Though voting almost certainly is not based on a single strand of thought – voting as a man, or as a skilled worker, or as a trade unionist, or as a young person – in the 1983 election Labour seemed to be offering trade unionists little. The Conservative Party, though, was offering union members power, by secret ballots, power to vote before going on strike, power to vote for union leaderships, power to vote on whether to maintain their union's political contributions. In 1983, the Conservatives lost only 2 per cent of the 10 per cent of union votes it had gained between 1974 and 1979. The Alliance seemed to represent consensus, and the birth of the SDP clearly helped push up the Liberal vote sharply by 13 percentage points from May 1979. Occupationally, only among non-skilled manual workers did Labour have half the available trade union vote. Among female trade unionists, the Labour vote was the same as the Conservative, and only just ahead of the Alliance. By region, the Conservatives had more of the union vote than Labour in the south, with the Alliance holding a share equal to Labour's (see Table 3.4).

Since the 1983 election, Labour's share of the trade union vote has improved, along with the overall proportion for the Party. But voting-intention figures are generally taken to include an element of protest against the Government, and so may be no clear indication of how the respondents would vote in a General Election. Similarly, the successful string of union votes to retain their political fund can hardly be taken as endorsements of the Labour Party, since apart from exceptions like Nupe and the AUEW the connection between the unions' funds and Labour was so little stressed as to be virtually invisible in the campaigns which preceded the voting in each union.

Table 3.4: *Trade union voting in the 1983 General Election (%)*

	Labour	*Conservative*	*Alliance*	*Total non-Labour*
By job				
White-collar	27	38	33	71
Skilled manual	44	27	27	54
Unskilled manual	50	25	24	49
By sex				
Men	41	29	28	57
Women	34	34	31	65
By region				
North and Scotland	44	26	28	54
Midlands and Wales	40	32	25	57
South	32	35	32	67

Source: MORI/TULV

Labour's loss of support among trade unionists – overall, among skilled and white-collar workers, among women, and in the south – marks a protracted change, as Whitty acknowledged: 'Many of these changes reflect long-term trends in sociological identification and attitudes of trade unionists to the Labour Party.' Though the level of trade union membership is roughly back now to what it was more than a decade ago, within that overall level the social and occupational mix of the workforce and of trade unions has changed radically: more white-collar workers, fewer blue-collar; more union members in national and local government, fewer in traditional heavy industries; more women, fewer men; more home-owners, fewer council tenants. Those marginalised into unemployment during the recession often have been semi- and unskilled workers; the workforce which remains is increasingly white-collar, increasingly home-owning.

Take, as an example, the miners. The shift towards home ownership among miners has been startling, whether or not it was eventually a factor during the strike – Scargill insisted it was not, and the sheer length of the strike bore him out, but the return to work suggested it was, and the primarily financial reasons given for the drift back support it. Nationally, the average figure for owner-occupancy is 61 per cent,[43] though among semi-skilled manual workers – demographically, roughly the miners' equivalent – the level is much lower, at 14.8 per cent. Regionally, in strong mining areas, the rate is lower too: 20.8 per cent in Yorkshire and Humberside, 10.9 per cent in the north. But in mining areas, owner-occupancy is considerably higher. Take the impressionistic evidence of Malcolm Green, manager at the start of the strike of the Halifax Building Society in Barnsley:

> Certainly we do get a large number of mortgage applications from people in the mining industry. It's a growing trend. Buying a house now is far more acceptable than was considered the norm. For the younger miner, there is a significant move away from the rented sector. Quite a few of the young miners who might have considered renting now consider buying their houses. They are earning good money and they are more prepared to go for a mortgage than their parents.

Or take the evidence of Bob Chalmers, Halifax assistant manager in Wigan: 'The miners are among the major wage earners in this area especially – their income is way over the average for the area. We do have a lot of mortgages at the moment from miners.' Figures bear out this anecdotal testimony. In Green's area, owner-occupancy is 47.2 per cent – much higher than the Yorkshire average; in Chalmers' it is 55.3 per cent. In Mansfield, at the heart of the Nottinghamshire coalfield, it is 57 per cent, and in the Rhondda it is among the highest in the country, at 76.1 per cent.[44]

Or take their politics. Archetypically, mining areas are those in which Labour votes are not counted, but weighed. In many, that is still the case. In 1983, there was a 13,848 majority for Labour in Bolsover, for instance, and of 14,190 in Hemsworth in West Yorkshire, both constituencies classed as mining seats, with more than 30 per cent of the population working in the industry. Whether the failure of the strike will have an impact in the next General Election remains to be seen, but there are already grave indications of this for Labour, as in the Nottinghamshire seat of Sherwood. Taking in five large pits, this new constituency seemed to have been created to provide a new seat for Labour. In the election, the unthinkable happened and the Conservative candidate squeezed in with a majority of 658. The formation of the breakaway Union of Democratic Mineworkers, and its incipient constitutional tussles with Labour, is likely to heighten the shift away from the Party. Speaking six months after the end of the strike, one miner, Alan Giles from Clipstone pit in north Notts, was scathing about Scargill's refusal to acknowledge social change. He said: 'Arthur Scargill's living in the age of the cloth cap and the greyhound on a piece of string, but the world's gone beyond that. The miners here have got washing machines, fitted carpets, and two televisions in their houses. Thirty years ago, you couldn't call your soul your own, but all that's changed now.'[45]

Scargill doubted it. 'There is a class consciousness,' he said of the miners, 'and whether they've got a new house, whoever builds it, and in whatever part of the nation it happens to be, mineworkers will be just as class-conscious as their forefathers.'[46] Perhaps they will; on the other hand, perhaps the outcome of the strike might change that (it might harden it, too). Scargill implies an immutability of class, unchanging values and experiences forming a constant consciousness. But, as Blackwell and Seabrook show so convincingly, the working class is protean, constantly remodelling itself. Even at the fundamental level where the test is what class people see themselves as belonging to, class is fluid, shifting from generation to generation (see Table 3.5): fewer seeing themselves as working class, more seeing themselves as shading towards the middle class. Such individual self-impressions of class position may not by themselves be a complete guide to any reshaping of class characteristics. This is partly because the standard definitions of class, based strongly on income, may be inadequate to describe a society in which pay differentials have shifted greatly (many 'white-collar' workers are paid less than many 'manual' workers, for instance), in which job contents have changed radically (why is a bus conductor classified as a manual worker when a VDU operator is not?),[47] and in which income is only one of a complex series of factors which delineate class.

Given such inadequacies, the redefinition of class suggested by Heath, Jowell and Curtice (1985) (HJC) is especially valuable. Instead of the standard classifications, they suggest this formulation of class:

Salariat (27 per cent of the electorate): managers, professionals, supervisors of non-manual workers.
Routine non-manual (24 per cent): clerks, salesworkers, secretaries.
Petty bourgeoisie (8 per cent): farmers, small proprietors, self-employed manual workers.

Table 3.5: *Self-perception of social class (%)*

	Self	*Parents*
Upper-middle	2	2
Middle	25	19
Upper-working	19	11
Working	48	59
Poor	3	8
Don't know	2	1

Source: R. Jowell and S. Witherspoon, *British Social Attitudes: The 1985 Report* (Aldershot, 1985)

Table 3.6: *Class voting in the 1983 General Election: normal classification (%)*

	Conservative	*Labour*	*Alliance*
AB (professional and managerial)	61	12	26
C1 (clerical)	55	21	24
C2 (skilled manual)	39	35	27
DE (semi- and unskilled)	29	44	28

Source: P. Kellner, 'Come Back Class Politics, All is Forgiven', *New Statesman*, 20 September 1985

Foremen and technicians (7 per cent): a blue-collar elite, whose supervisory functions set them apart from most manual workers.
Working class (34 per cent): general manual workers, including skilled employees, sometimes highly paid, but generalised by being subject to detailed supervision at work.[48]

Under this scheme, class depends not on income levels but on general economic interests. It radically redraws the political map. Table 3.6 shows the 1983 General Election interpreted along normal lines of class definition. Table 3.7 demonstrates the same result under the HJC classification. It presents some remarkable conclusions: variations in support for all parties are greater than normally seems

Table 3.7: *Class voting in the 1983 General Election: Heath, Jowell, Curtice classification (%)*

	Conservative	*Labour*	*Alliance*
Petty bourgeoisie	71	12	17
Salariat	54	14	31
Foremen/technicians	48	26	25
Routine non-manual	46	25	27
Working class	30	49	20

Source: A. Heath, R. Jowell and J. Curtice, *How Britain Votes* (Oxford, 1985)

to be the case under the usual classification; Conservative support is greatest not among the professional classes, but among the entrepreneurial petty bourgeoisie, whose advancement the Conservative Government has elevated into a political fetish; the Alliance's support is spread across the classes.

But it is the implications of the HJC reclassification for the structure of the working class which are important here. One influential model of class realignment[49] sees class as a declining force in social characteristics and attitudes, even though opinion surveys do not bear this out (Jowell and Witherspoon 1985, for example, found that 63 per cent of those surveyed considered class to matter to a great or considerable extent, and that class is surprisingly stable as a social force, mostly neither declining in the last ten years nor likely to do so in the next ten). Against this trend, the HJC analysis reinstates class, *but in a different form*. Its reappraisal of the 1983 election, for instance, shows Labour, in what was clearly a particularly bad election for the Party, retaining half the working-class vote. But crucially, under this analysis the working class is a declining segment of the electorate (47 per cent in 1964, 34 per cent two decades later). Moreover, among the 'technicians and foremen' segment, Labour scores badly, with the Conservatives holding a significant lead. HJC conclude that 'the Labour Party is certainly not the party of the blue-collar elite.'[50]

The split of the high-tech employees from traditional working-class perceptions and attitudes is further apparent when the HJC 'salariat' classification is sub-divided into 'managers in small establishments' and 'ancillary workers' – semi-professionals including computer programmers and technicians. These are to the left of the small managers, with a much lower Conservative vote (44 per cent, compared with 68 per cent); but the Conservative vote is still dominant, with 35 per cent voting for the Alliance and only 19 per cent for Labour.

What this seems to indicate, then, is that the idea of a 'new' working class can be given substance, albeit with caution: new working classes have been discovered before, only to dissolve even as their discoverers define them. That may happen here, too. As the Labour Party reshapes itself, with its constituent parts having no other choice but to support the new presidential style of leadership of Neil Kinnock if they are to retain any hope of winning elections, it makes itself more attractive, perhaps drawing back to itself its old supporters. But perhaps not; the changes in the working class which voting figures indicate may well imply the fashioning of a new, different form of employee – with different material values, different attitudes, different ambitions, different ideological views. Translated into the world of work, these changes indicate a more flexible, more consensual approach. Among the industrial changes which these new attitudes have wrought against an almost wholly altered economic background, few have probably been so far-reaching as those which have swept through the employees' representative organisations – the trade unions.

Trade Unions

'It's a couple of quid a month going to I don't know who, I don't know what it's doing, and I don't think a union can really help me anyway. It's the first time I've worked, and I haven't done anything wrong, and I don't think I will.' This is a teenage girl, an employee in a high-tech factory. This is another: 'I haven't joined the union because I didn't really know much about it when I was at school, really, but I came here and all you hear about on the television is strikes and demonstrations, and I thought, you know, I don't really want to bother with that, so I didn't bother joining, because there's too much argument. I'd rather just be here to work, do my job and go home in the evening.'[51] It is not a left-led union with a militant stance, like Tass, which they have spurned. The only union they could join at their plant, with its single-union deal, is one with a moderate, responsible, image, the EETPU.

In Ipswich, a 1984 survey by the local chamber of commerce found that fewer than 20 per cent of teenage schoolchildren wanted to join a union when they started work. In a survey of young people in Gwent taken at the same time, fewer than half could see any positive benefits from trade unionism. According to MORI, strong trade unionism is seen as important to workers' employment security by only 19 per cent of those surveyed in late 1985 – fewer among young people (15 per cent), fewer again among young men (14 per cent), fewer still among young women (10 per cent): very little seedcorn here, small prospect in the future for unions of strength growing from commitment.

What all this shows is not that people do not like trade unions (poll evidence indicates that high points of trade union unpopularity, of a feeling that unions have too much power, tend to coincide with large, high-profile strikes: the 1978–9 winter of discontent, the

1984–5 miners' strike); what it shows is that on the whole people just do not care: unions are not important to them, not really in their frame of thinking, an irrelevance. For unions battered by the recession, after a tough few years of it since the Conservative Government came to power, this is a hard message to listen to. TUC membership has fallen in the period 1979–84 by 19 per cent – more than 2.3 million. A union such as the TGWU, which has seen more than half a million of its members disappear, has lost more members in the period than most unions in even their wildest dreams would ever hope to have. Unions have tried to stop the rot, by amalgamation, by streamlining their organisations, by recruitment, and membership decline now seems to have slowed, though that may mean no more than that the unions are down to their bedrock level, where their membership consists of employees with check-off arrangements, under which the employer automatically deducts union subscriptions at source, effectively maintaining union membership rolls.

Some union leaders argue that the 1970s was an abnormal period for unions, with membership levels at a peculiarly high level, and that now the norm is reasserting itself. Perhaps so; but against that, trade union density – the proportion of the working population who are union members – is declining. The number of union members is falling, while the number of employees in work is slightly rising. The unions are not keeping pace. TUC density stood in 1985 at 46.3 per cent, overall trade union density, taking into account non-TUC unions, a little higher. That is if the figures are correct: with few computerised membership records (though the requirement in the 1984 Trade Union Act for unions to compile central members' registers will change that, eventually), many unions' claimed memberships have been little more than vague, half-hopeful estimates. Far from 46 per cent being union members, poll evidence in the 1985 British social attitudes survey suggests that only 26 per cent are in membership.[52]

But that survey also shows that unions are recognised at 63 per cent of workplaces, and this suggests two conclusions. First, it may indicate that participation in trade unionism is very low. MORI poll evidence bears this out: it reveals union activists to be highly involved in their unions, attending meetings, putting forward resolutions, voting. The level of participation overall in union affairs is low, clearly because trade union density is less than half the population – reflected in the poll sample. But the level of participation by union members again demonstrates a lack of interest, a view of unions as not very relevant. Even among union members, only 30 per cent thought belonging to a strong union was important for their job security.[53]

Secondly, one may conclude that non-unionism is high. And why not? Employees tend to join unions for a complex variety of reasons – such as because they have been a union member before, or because their family or friends are or have been; because they actively want to; because they don't actively not want to; because a union is effective in recruiting them; because an employer is; because they are moved, intellectually or emotionally, by the moral force of union membership. The pull of that force now seems lessened: picket lines, as the concrete embodiment of that force, no longer hold sway as they used to, as the miners' strike demonstrated so vividly. Another reason, an important one, is self-interest: what protection can a union give me, what strength, what services, what advantages, what leverage? In the 1970s, when unions were seen to be strong – however unreal that strength might actually have been – the issue did not arise: employers mostly did not test to extremes the assumption of ready collective force to promote and support a series of demands. But now, weakened, much of their economic muscle gone, the unions' ability to deliver for their members, to secure achievements for them by virtue of their membership, is lessened. The pay differential between union membership and non-membership is now marginal: recent research at Warwick University suggests that the present difference is very small, mostly in single figures – a 10 per cent lead for semi-skilled manual workers who are union members, 4 per cent for middle managers, 3 per cent for clerical workers and only 1 per cent for skilled manuals.[54]

So why should people bother to join, or remain in, a union? In addition to their function of protecting or even advancing jobs, wages and conditions, unions have a role rather like that of a friendly society, providing benefits for members. With the level of social provision now made by the state – a level achieved, at least in part, through the unions' own political efforts – many benefits offered by unions are virtually redundant. Gavin Laird, general secretary of the engineering workers' union, tried to drop some of his union's benefits which both duplicated those of the state and were dwarfed by them; but in the tradition-bound AUEW, a member took the union to court to prevent the move – and won. Some unions offer more than traditional benefits: the non-TUC Professional Association of Teachers offers free insurance to its members, covering such issues important to teachers as vandal damage to their cars during school time and loss of private property while at school. In addition it provides an extensive discount scheme, providing reductions on a range of products, from holidays to computers, from frozen food to gas cookers. John Andrews, PAT assistant general secretary, acknowledges that no one is likely to join the union for the benefits it offers, but he claims that they are more likely to remain in membership once they have seen what the union can make available.

Shifting towards competition with organisations like the AA in offering a range of services might for many unions seem too humbling a role, too insignificant a part to play in people's lives. Clearly, in their concerted knowledge, experience and expertise, unions can offer advantages to employees – some of them intangible, others less so. They are obviously a long way from convincing many of their own members, let alone non-members – especially not those employed in new areas, on new work, with new ideas and new attitudes – of the merit of their case. But it is significant that they have realised that. They are trying, as Norman Willis, TUC general secretary, puts it:

> For a long time, many sectors of the trade union movement seemed, perhaps, to have life relatively easy. In the '60s and '70s there was a natural recruitment pool, regularly topped up, and most unions could expand without perhaps having to worry unduly about the best ways to attract and retain new members. No one believes that to be the case any more.

Or, as his deputy, Ken Graham, says: 'We can't just work on the assumption now that trade unions are a good idea – why don't you join us?'

4

New Realism in the Unions

Broadway in London is a far cry from New York's theatreland. A Whitehall tributary, it is the home of the headquarters of London Transport and of the Council of Civil Service Unions; their close neighbours include the Home Office, the Department of Employment and New Scotland Yard. It is also the national address of the largest single-sector employers' body in the country – the Engineering Employers' Federation. On 10 June 1983, Dr James McFarlane, the EEF's director-general, who laces his 'tough employer' stance with flashes of bone-dry humour, hosted a reception for an EEF staffer who was leaving the organisation. In the wake of the Conservatives' sweeping General Election victory, finally confirmed early that morning, euphoria would have been understandable, even expected. But the dominant mood was unconcern: 'I didn't stay up to watch,' said one employer. 'What was the point?' For the employers, none: so sure were they of the Conservatives' victory that well before the election there was no longer any real doubt.

That assurance could hardly have contrasted more sharply with the gloomy prophecies of trade union leaders on the election TV specials. Hoping against hope, turning their eyes from the clear signs before them – the Conservatives ebullient, still riding the wake of victory in the Falklands war; a third party splitting the opposition vote; a Labour Party deeply divided behind a bewildered and uninspiring Michael Foot – Britain's union leaders had pinned their all on the return of another Labour Government. However bad had been the last four years, however hard their power and their impact had been hit by the recession, the prospect of Labour righting it all had kept them warm in trade unionism's wintry days in the early 1980s.

Suddenly, that was gone. Suddenly, they had to face the real prospect: another term of office for a Government so implacably and ideologically opposed to the unions that at best it was dismissively, humiliatingly indifferent to them, a Government newly revitalised by electoral success, its franchise – a still-crucial part of it devoted to curtailing the power of the trade unions – freshly invigorated. Perhaps worst of all, they had to face the fact that the largest-ever proportion of their own members had spurned the unions' virtually unanimous collective advice to support Labour. Even a quarter of the unemployed, who, Labour and the unions had argued passionately, had most to lose from the Conservatives had voted for the Government. Gloomy they may have been in the television studios; on the whole, it was the best they could manage. For many, it masked near-despair.

'Still fresh in our minds', said Alistair Graham, the then general secretary of the civil servants' union CPSA at the annual TUC Congress less than three months later, 'is the spectacle of policies which have been developed and refined by Congress over many years being rejected in a general election by the people of this country on a scale which many of us find difficult to comprehend.'[1] Difficult as it was, the TUC Congress that year presented starkly to Britain's beleaguered trade unions two options, mutually exclusive, each containing in itself the denial of the other. In Blackpool, the start of the miners' overtime ban which prefaced the 1984–5 strike was weeks away, and for Arthur Scargill, NUM president, the die was already well cast. He warned the Congress apocalyptically:

> Once again, today our industry faces the axe as the Tory Government and the Coal Board both advance menacingly with a closure programme of 70 pits and 70,000 jobs. Not only did British Steel have to endure Ian McGregor, but they have sent him to wreak his vengeance on the British coal industry. They are determined, irrespective of the facts, to close down at least 70 pits, and the economics of the industry are no longer being considered.[2]

Scargill's call to the Congress to 'recognise its responsibility' went unheeded; his warning that 'You do not obtain the best for your membership by going to talk to someone whose intention is to execute you. The only thing that you can talk about is the means of execution,' was rejected. Indeed, Graham – much to his acute embarrassment when the coal strike actually began – even drew a burst of applause from the packed delegates when he taunted Scargill and the miners, saying 'Some of us are waiting till he gets them out on a decent industrial dispute.' But his mockery was understandable. That year, the TUC ran his way: revolutionary vanguardism was rejected; sober reflection, cool analysis, sophisticated theory were embraced. 'New realism', the industrial correspondents dubbed it, to the irritation of the then-TUC general secretary, Len Murray: but it fitted, and it stuck.

New Realism at Blackpool

Three men characterised the 1983 TUC – Frank Chapple, that year's TUC chairman; Murray, the general secretary; and Alistair Graham. All three are to the right in trade union affairs, Chapple formidably so. Two, Chapple and Murray, have since taken life peerages, and now sit in the House of Lords. For their opponents, nothing else could be more conclusive proof of their treachery. While the sheer scale of the electorate's rejection of the policies proposed by Labour and the unions kept those opponents more subdued at Blackpool in 1983 than usual, they were still there, still vocal, and their criticisms have grown since. Graham's left-wing critics in his own union, the Civil and Public Services Association, which at its leadership and activist level is deeply and irrevocably divided on political lines, were triumphant when, in spring 1986, Graham resigned from the union to head the Industrial Society.

Chapple, a squat barrel of a man, combined a near-fanatical anti-Communism (often characteristic of former Party members) with both intellectual courage (sometimes, necessarily, physical courage too) and overt aggression. He further coupled all this with a deep-seated belief, almost uncannily justified by events, in his ability to reflect his own members' wishes. At Blackpool he set the dominant tone for the week by grabbing the issue of the unions' collapse in credibility by the scruff of its neck, and shaking it. In his keynote presidential address, he told the Congress:

> For more than 20 years our popularity has been sliding. At the same time, many of our members have been expressing their unease. This unease has not all been simply whipped up by right-wing newspapers or manufactured by opinion pollsters. It has also reflected itself in the mass desertion of Labour votes and the support which this Government's industrial relations legisla-

> tion has attracted. It is crucially important that our movement recognises these criticisms. If we had listened earlier, we might not have suffered the catastrophe of June 9, or the defeat of five years ago.[3]

Bitter medicine to swallow; and while he carefully eased it down by tracing in outline the impact on the unions of the economy, of unemployment and of the Government's 'irrelevant' free-market beliefs, he left no doubts about the challenge the unions themselves had to face, to deal with, if they were to survive:

> The working-class movement that is being fashioned by recession, new technology, 40 years of a welfare state and ever-developing aspirations, is profoundly different from that in which most of us grew up. In a few years' time women will constitute nearly half of the workforce; industry will be more concentrated in the south-east; a larger number of our members will be home-owners, new skills will have replaced the ones we know. If British trade unionism is to avoid the mistakes which have weakened our colleagues in other countries, we have to adapt to these changes and provide the kind of movement that they imply. We will have to stop wishing that the world was like it once was, and face up to what it is.

Chapple's call for the unions to 'appeal to the new working class, and not cling to old-fashioned definitions of 50 years ago' clearly struck a chord, reflecting the prevailing mood, and enhancing it. From the *Sun* to the *Guardian*, his call won approval. Chapple himself later summed up the response: ordinary people were saying to him, 'Thank God someone is talking sense at last. They're not all mad at the TUC after all.'[4]

Murray's speech, two days later, was less aggressive, but no less passionate – unusually so for Murray, a careful, controlled, thoughtful man, honed by his own Methodist beliefs and a lifetime in Congress House into an orthodoxy which his critics saw as rigidity, but which his stance at Blackpool in 1983 and over the NGA's Warrington dispute with Eddie Shah demonstrated was real leadership. 'The employers have not got the answers,' he said, 'and the Government obviously has not got the answers, and we have not yet convinced our members that we have. We cannot just say that our policies are fine and that it is our members who are all wrong.'

For the left in the unions and in the Labour Party, this had in fact been the explanation for Labour's defeat. Murray was having none of it. Many union members had not found the Conservative Government intolerable:

> They have voted, and we respect that. We cannot talk as if the trade union movement is some sort of alternative government, Brother Bonnie Prince Charlie waiting to be summoned back from exile. We are representative organisations, and being representative means knowing and respecting what our members want and expect from their unions – not the Government's unions, not the Labour Party's unions, not even our unions, but the members' unions.[5]

Both Murray and Chapple laid stress on the need for unions to talk to governments if they were to exert any influence at all. With a Conservative Government in power this was, for some, bad enough: Graham went further. Or rather, he seemed to: 'This motion', he felt the need to tell the Congress in proposing a wholesale review of the principles of modern trade unionism, 'is not, as some have argued, about ditching the Labour Party.'[6] Graham, unusually for trade union general secretaries, who face enormous demands on their time, is still an active member of his local south London Labour Party branch. And within weeks of the Blackpool Congress, his union tried, unsuccessfully, to persuade its members to vote in favour of re-affiliation with Labour. One of the new breed of younger union leaders, Graham was suspected by some in his polarised union of being pro-SDP – a suspicion confirmed in their minds when in 1985 he spoke at fringe meetings at the Conservative, Liberal and Social Democratic Party conferences, but not at Labour's (in fact, he had spoken there the previous year).

Graham's resolution to the 1983 Congress was extraordinary, not just for its analytical approach, rare enough on any conference rostrum, let alone the TUC's, but primarily simply for being there. Increasingly, TUC resolutions had become mere bags of words, sounding well but signifying little. Arthur Scargill in 1984 was to confront the TUC with living up to a rhetoric which its principals knew was phoney; Graham took another course twelve months earlier, and faced the TUC with some crucial questions. Why had union members failed to support TUC and Labour policies? Were the policies wrong? Why were young people turned off by the TUC?

How could the unions prosper? What, indeed, were they for? Such reappraisals are common enough in business, but in the TUC, where the conservative momentum is usually of near-irresistible proportions, this was radical stuff. 'We are at a watershed in our affairs,' Graham said. 'It is obvious that very many of us are in the mood for change, and my argument is that change we must.'

High unemployment, falling union membership, dropping union density, Graham spelt out the scale of the unions' difficulties, and rejected the argument that the problem was the teller, not the tale. 'If we adopt that analysis' – chosen by the hard left, and chosen again, significantly, by the Conservative Party in late 1985 as its own electoral fortunes seemed to be sliding – 'it is much more likely that we shall be trapped into a slow, miserable decline as our members vote with their feet.' He won through, convincing a Congress that wanted to be won over:

> We need to change attitudes. We need to change policies. We need to restore idealism to our movement, which is why the motion suggests a statement of principles on modern trade unionism. Let's face it, in the last general election there was a massive credibility gap. On the one hand, we wanted to foist radical prescriptions on many groups of people, involving change for many British institutions. Yet on the other hand, the public perceived us to be timid and conservative about reforming ourselves. Where we were involved in unpalatable commitments, such as the income side of the National Economic Assessment, we tended to use weasel words to fudge that commitment so that the electorate had to be theologians to understand what it all meant. We must approach a review of principles, policies and the determination of priorities that this motion involves with a genuine humility, with a readiness to listen to our members as well as our activists. The policies have to have an impact on our members' lives in a way that they will support.

Not everyone agreed. Alex Kitson, the gritty, Scottish deputy general secretary of the giant Transport and General Workers' Union, called it devious. Ann Field, of the general print union Sogat '82, shuddered at the prospect of a 'retreat into the dark ages'. Jimmy Knapp of the NUR argued that the unions should not run away from their socialist aims. In the event, the prevailing mood was shown to be against them: by 5.8 million to 4 million votes, Graham's review was instigated. New realism was born.

TUC Strategy

Stripped of its influence in Whitehall, finding little solace in its generally ineffective demonstrations in Trafalgar Square, the TUC in the 1980s has found itself in search of a role. Coupled with the loss of some of its more powerful leaders – Jack Jones of the transport workers, Hugh Scanlon of the engineers – this has pushed it towards its own crisis of authority. For most union members, the TUC in any case has always seemed remote, rarefied. The Conservative Government's successful drive to demonstrate the gap that had opened between leaders and members shifted the focus of this lack of interest from membership to leadership level. Under this scrutiny, the TUC revealed only disunity: there was Arthur Scargill's abandonment of a TUC General Council place after just a year of service, which acted as a kind of preface to the NUM's six-month-long refusal even to involve the TUC in the most major industrial dispute since the 1926 General Strike; there were the decisions by a number of unions, led by the AUEW and the EETPU, to counter TUC policy directly on the high-profile issue of accepting Government money to fund internal ballots; and there was the widespread and equally flagrant disregard by virtually every TUC union for TUC policy on the less publicity-sensitive matters of closed-shop ballots and participation in industrial tribunals.

Such public reverses for the TUC hit it, and hit it hard. Even so, its root talent was still there, if strained: its ability, born from long years of practice, of seeing the way through, finding a compromise, doing a deal. For the TUC, the Graham motion at the Blackpool Congress was a welcome challenge, and a source of trouble at the same time. Opposition was inevitable, facing up to the issue equally unavoidable. Normally, the TUC's much-leaked position papers, covering the whole range of issues with which it deals, tend to be written, sometimes at a quite junior level, by one or at most two of its small team of often young, mostly recently graduated and overworked officials. Department heads – principally organisation, economic, international, social insurance, education and information – give to the documents the approval of the TUC office before they are passed on for scrutiny by their appropriate committees and finally by the full General Council. Often, the TUC's departments are quite disparate, keen to protect their own areas of interest and influence. Putting the strategy resolution into effect was a quite different affair. Though the final statement bore the joint imprimatur of Murray and Roy Jackson, then head of the education department but promoted since the strategy exercise to assistant general secretary, the sheer sweep of the subject effectively demanded a fully co-operative effort.

The result, when it first appeared in draft form at the beginning of 1984, was startling – the most forthright and thorough-going self-examination the unions had carried out since their evidence to the Donovan Commission on industrial relations in the mid-1960s. 'Unions must prove their fitness to play a continuing role in the future,'[7] the document stated in its opening passages. It was rooted in present practice: 'The basic principles of trade unionism are relevant to the 1980s. Trade union objectives do not need revising – they still need implementing: and trade unions will continue to seek change through collective bargaining and through political influence.' But its thrust for change was at least as strong, probably stronger: 'Trade unions cannot survive on yesterday's achievements.'

What was notable about TUC Strategy was that – unusually for unions in the 1980s – it did not duck the key issues; did not even try to. Opinion-poll evidence had for years shown a conflict of attitudes towards the unions. Many people still saw something of value in unions – in the abstract. But on almost every particular issue, especially that of trade union power, the unions were found sorely wanting. Crucially, the TUC paper saw public support as indivisible from the issue of membership involvement: its members *were* the public who opposed what the unions had been doing, the public its members.

'Membership participation in some aspects of union affairs is less satisfactory than in others,' the TUC said. Branch meetings, which typically attract fewer than 5 per cent of members, had become almost like Victorian rotten boroughs, in the worst cases, especially where they are linked, as in the GMBATU or the NUR, with a block-vote system. (A branch meeting decides which candidate to support in an election; the entire numerical vote of the branch is then firmly pledged for that contender, no matter how few of the branch's total membership attended the election meeting.)

The Conservative Government had sought, largely successfully, to emphasise such gaps between members and their leaders, at whatever level, as the TUC recognised: 'It is the case in many unions, whatever their constitutional arrangements, that the average member's interest is mostly limited to what occurs at his or her place of work, and, by and large, the member is content for the minority to carry on with the work necessary to ensure the continuing functioning of the union.' The TUC held out no magic potion for reviving flagging trade union branch life; it simply accepted that a branch divorced from the workplace could appear less relevant to union members. Not that workplace representativeness was ideal: as the TUC noted in connection with its estimate of the 300,000 shop stewards or their equivalent in British unions, 'it would appear that in too many cases the pressure on the representative's time has been at the expense of contact with the members.'

Extending the argument, the TUC also saw problems in the unions' 4000-strong full-time officer corps, suggesting that in the light of industrial change, officers were often now simply located in the wrong place, and had experience in traditional plants which might no longer be relevant to the new areas of employment. 'Recruitment strategies often cannot be based on past union experience. The way unions mount recruitment campaigns might often need to be reviewed to reflect the different employment circumstances in new industries.' Such new industries were seen as vital for future organisation, though the document also identified other possible areas for growth: in the large unorganised pockets in manufacturing, particularly in white-collar, technical and professional grades; in the private service sector; among women, the young, the unemployed, the ethnic minorities, and – least plausibly – the self-employed.

'Management have sought to secure changes in working methods and technology, if necessary by imposing them,' the TUC said. 'The belief in management by consent – dominant in many large companies during the 1970s – has lessened and, in its place, more aggressive and assertive management styles have developed.' That was likely to continue: 'the tendency may be for technological change and the reduction in the demand for labour to continue to strengthen the employers' position rather than that of the employees.'

Trade Unions and the Labour Party

Probably what was most surprising about TUC Strategy was not what it said – its analysis, though sharp, was not new – but the fact that it said it at all. It presented the TUC's unions with difficult choices: modify or melt away, change or collapse. But it also contained a get-out, which the left seized upon. Its forty-two closely packed pages contained only eighteen lines devoted to the unions and Labour, and what it said in those two paragraphs was loose and unspecific. Some of the initiative's major proponents did not help its cause in this sense, either. John Lyons, of the EMA, took an openly cool line towards Labour in his Hitachi lecture. 'The TUC should certainly retain its special relationship with the Labour Party,' he said.[8] 'I am sure that all the individual unions affiliated to the Labour Party will do so anyway.' But Lyons argued that the TUC's link with Labour had become so close that the TUC looked like losing its independence; the TUC was being used as part of the Party's own internal power struggle. 'It is simply not possible for the TUC to put all its eggs in the Labour Party basket,' he said. 'It knows . . . that the likelihood of the Labour Party being returned as the majority party at the next election in 1987 or 1988 is very remote.' Accordingly, the course for the TUC – 'reasonably clear, and relatively uncontroversial' – was for it to 'enter into discussions with other parties in the country which might form a future government, or be part of a future government', including possibly the Scottish, Welsh and Ulster parties, but principally and particularly the Liberal–SDP Alliance. Lyons made manifest his views when at the end of 1985 he became the first-ever union general secretary and TUC General Council member to join the SDP.

Even before such a dramatic move, Lyons' kind of talk was more than enough for the left. The SDP had already started to make moves towards the trade unions by appointing a trade union officer, Tony Halmos, adding insult to injury, as the union left saw it, by recruiting him from within the TUC's own organisation department. Trade union involvement with the SDP was slow to make ground; until Lyons' declaration, John Grant, head of communications at the EETPU electricians' union, and Mike Blick, a senior lay official in Nalgo, were the Party's most prominent public supporters in the unions. Official union suspicion of the SDP, which was not confined to the left, was confirmed when the Party began to take a close interest in the 1985–6 political fund ballots required under the 1984 Act, and in the ballot-rigging allegations which clouded the general secretaryship and executive elections in the TGWU in 1985. In fact, the startling success of the unions' campaign on political funds saw off the SDP at a very early stage; after initial newspaper advertisements during the first ballot, that of the print union Sogat '82, the party effectively withdrew from the arena, sensing correctly which way the wind was blowing. The Government was taken aback by the string of substantial votes in favour of retaining the political funds which the unions' campaign produced. The campaign was guided by the wily Bill Keys, ex-Sogat general secretary and a veteran of countless internal union manoeuvres, and by Graham Allen, a former GLC official, who together blended a new subtlety of approach with a near-tireless determination to deal with any problem which might prevent victory in the ballots. By the campaign, the unbroken success of the votes was one of the unions' most impressive achievements of recent years, seeing victories not just in such obviously pro-Labour unions as the TGWU or GMBATU, but even in those which had been in doubt, like the film technicians' ACTT or the white-collar ASTMS. The success of the political fund campaign defied the logic and intention of that part of the 1984 Act which governed the funds: the unions' links with Labour were strengthened, their own internal politics often virtually rediscovered, and their very structures re-examined and reinforced.

New Realism: Union Responses

In a sense, what the left saw as the secret tendency of the new realism towards middle-ground, non-Labour politics gave it both an opportunity to oppose TUC Strategy, and a respite from its challenge. What was clear was that its sheer breadth made it difficult for unions – and not just those on the left – to handle. Take the TUC's largest affiliate, the left-led TGWU. Its confidential response to the TUC took the issue head on, but then shrugged off its analysis:

> The introduction of the document presupposes that there is a crisis (or at least serious problems) in the union movement because of declining membership, reduced bargaining power, a poor public image and status, the widening gap between the union and individual members and a poor relationship with Government. Some of this is true, some is exaggerated, but whatever the case it should be made crystal clear that the cause of these problems is not the internal structure of trade unions. It is the result of the economic slump and the hostility of Government.[9]

Arguing that the strategy paper 'mixes together major issues of sweeping changes of policy with specific questions which are by comparison trivial', the TGWU in its response to it struck the very same note, uneasily blending what were at the time dominant issues on the union left such as tripartism (co-operating with organisations like the MSC, Acas and the NEDC) and the Government's labour legislation with sketchy points about the new industries or about bargaining in the recession.[10] From the centre-right, comments from GMBATU were equally disappointing: a rehearsal of the industrial and social changes examined in the strategy paper, followed by a discussion of the union's particular points of interest, such as a financial audit of union activities.[11]

Nupe recognised the need to present a positive case for trade unionism, but contented itself with little strategic change: 'Our view on the role of trade unions is summed up in one sentence of the TUC's strategy paper: "Trade union objectives do not need revising – they need implementing."'[12] But if Nupe did not take up the opportunity offered by the TUC, it was nonetheless considering carefully how best to implement those objectives. Rodney Bickerstaffe, its young, attractive and charismatic general secretary, is now, on conference platforms, the public face of the union – emotive, powerful, determined, caring. But working with him is his deputy, Tom Sawyer, a former regional officer for the union in the north-east. Now a crucial member of the inside left on the Labour Party's national executive committee, it is Sawyer who has chiefly promoted the union's thinking. Like Bickerstaffe, he was a vociferous opponent of new realism, which was allowed by its proponents to be seen as collaboration with a hated Government. But Sawyer picked up its principal strands of thought:

> There was and remains a need for a debate on the future of the trade unions. The changing nature of the workforce, the government's hostility and the challenge of ballots on political funds, the need to find a convincing response to major issues like mass unemployment, all make it essential for the trade unions to rethink their purpose and methods.[13]

Sawyer saw the strength of trade unions as deriving from their membership, and he urged involvement, and beyond that recruitment – 'unglamorous, but vital' – and not just at activist level: 'No more can we rely on elected activists exercising their mandates without the necessary and continuous involvement of their members.' Nupe, with a large proportion of female members, started putting into practice the ideas generated by those members: more informal, relaxed union meetings; rotating branch-level trade union offices, to give members experience; pressing for time off with pay for union meetings; providing transport to them; holding them in places other than in clubs and pubs, and at times convenient for working women, and men, to get to.

The NUR, too, responded actively to the TUC Strategy, accepting the opportunity to be candid. But then, even before the refusal of its London Underground members to heed their leaders' call to strike in 1985 without a ballot, it had good reason. Referring to a national strike aborted after less than a day, the union declared:

> We learned our lesson the hard way. In June 1982, when the call went out for industrial action, the army, which we had always assumed would be ready to march, was simply not there. The issues had not been properly explained, the organisation at district and branch level was very patchy and in many cases non-existent and perhaps for the first time we became aware of the degree of alienation between the union and its policy and the views of our members.[14]

Because of that chastening experience, which at that stage few other unions had faced, the NUR was positive, detailing its own organisational changes, welcoming the TUC's move, realising the scale of the problems confronting the unions – and not trying to shift the blame:

> We should not be surprised when many of our members turn away from their traditional loyalties to us and the Labour movement. We have done little to win their confidence in our ability to handle their day to day problems at work, we have become too remote – relying on the employer to hand out the membership forms and to collect the money for us. Why should we expect them to follow our lead?

This was tough talking for the opponents of change to combat, precisely because it came from a union on the left, with a proud and militant history – one which was to display itself again in the support it gave, almost alone among the TUC's unions, to the NUM during the miners' strike. In some unions, the response to events charted by TUC Strategy was more concrete.

Take Britain's third-largest union, the GMBATU. John Edmonds, an Oxford-educated bookbinder's son, took over on 1 January 1986, as its general secretary. For long widely seen as the very model of the new union leader – professional, analytical, strong on organisation, but also (as the employers with whom he has dealt will testify) a strong and successful negotiator – his rise to the top seemed almost inevitable. In a strong field, Edmonds had scored a landslide victory in the election for the general secretaryship – out of a total vote of about 700,000, Edmonds was almost 120,000 votes in front of the whole of the rest of the candidates combined. To passionate applause from union activists in a Blackpool hotel in September 1985, Edmonds spelt out carefully and cogently what his victory would mean for the union. Fundamentally, he saw the need for unions to campaign for all working people, not just for those in membership; in effect he was abandoning the sectionalist point of view which had both sustained unions and come to cripple them.

More than most union leaders, Edmonds has described, analysed and tried to come to terms with the harsh changes which have hit the unions in the 1980s. He has detailed the shift of unemployment from its limited and regional origins to its present widespread and national character, the impact of redundancies, the move from manufacturing to service work, the disappearance of single-product companies, the shrinking of factory size: 'The effect of the recession', he wrote, 'has been to compress 20 years of structural change into the lifetime of two parliaments.'[15] His view is that 'trade unions cannot hope to represent unhappy and fragmented groups of members with the techniques that served well enough in the big integrated factories of the 1960s.'

Since taking over from David Basnett, Edmonds has started to forge his own version of the new unionism, putting some of these ideas into practice. Backed by a new team of David Warburton, an influential figure on the Labour Party right and now effectively the GMBATU's deputy general secretary, and flanked by Alan Cave, one of the TUC's most able backroom specialists as head of research (the job Larry Whitty left to become Labour's general secretary), Edmonds is likely to make the union a testbed for some of his ideas about how unions need to operate in the 1980s. On becoming general secretary, for instance, Edmonds commissioned a study of employment in Britain in the 1990s, as a basis for the union's recruitment and amalgamation strategy. Hardly radical, you might think, but it was an approach not properly considered before by UK unions – attempting to provide a solid foundation for membership expansion. But Edmonds saw it, and his job, as more than that, as less self-interested – he was seeking to identify areas where 'there was a great need for union protection'. He started his job with his own new unionism, his own self-made agenda:

> For six years the trade union movement has been obsessed with the task of defending its rights and structures against a hostile government. During that time, we have spent too much time looking inward at ourselves. Too often we have given the impression that we are only interested in defending the privileges of a few union leaders. We have looked selfish and self-centred. In defending trade unions, we have sometimes appeared to have forgotten working people.

Edmonds and GMBATU are managing to change. But many unions either wilfully, or by default, managed to avoid the challenge presented by industrial change and set out in TUC Strategy – at least at the formal, public level. But they did this not by mustering successful opposition against it; in 1983 issues were stirring which were soon to show that they did not need even to do that. The challenge of change was met not internally, by the unions themselves, but externally, by events.

New Realism Discredited: GCHQ

The searching questions posed at the 1983 Congress, and codified in the TUC Strategy document, posed a major challenge to Britain's unions, and offered them the opportunity of revitalising themselves to meet the complex and more hostile pattern of industrial relations in the 1980s. In a sense, it was what the Conservative Government had been pushing for. It was all the more surprising, then – or all the more expected, to those who saw the Government as straightforwardly anti-union – that it was a decision by a Conservative Government which dealt the new mood the first, and undoubtedly the heaviest, of the twin blows it was to suffer almost at birth.

Three days before Christmas 1983, the decision was taken – though ironically enough, few outside the Cabinet Room in 10

Downing Street knew of it on that December day. Nothing leaked out; there were no lobby briefings to the handful of political journalists still half-heartedly on duty in the depths of the Parliamentary recess. For their counterparts in the industrial correspondents' corps, 25 January looked little better: the major diary event looked set to be the tabling in the Department of Health and Social Security's shabby south London headquarters of a new-style pay claim for ambulance workers, which reflected both the growing impact on industrial relations in the ambulance service of the non-TUC professional association for ambulance staffs, and the general mood of realism which was also edging the negotiators for much of the rest of hospital employment towards a new, long-term pay agreement including new guidelines for limiting industrial action to protect patients.

But on the afternoon of 25 January, the private became public. When Sir Geoffrey Howe, Foreign Secretary, rose to make what was billed as an announcement on 'GCHQ and the Employment Protection Acts' no one had any idea of what was coming. Mild interest, but little more than that – how could the Employment Protection Acts be interesting? – was stirred only among those who knew what GCHQ was: Government Communications Headquarters, the main official listening post, based at Cheltenham in Gloucestershire (with a string of outstations up and down the country, plus a few abroad), of the Government's security and intelligence services. In other words, the main spy centre.

Howe's statement was short, but astonishing. With immediate effect, the unfair dismissal and other provisions of the 1970s Employment Protection Acts were being removed from staff at GCHQ. New conditions of service were also being introduced: 'Under those new conditions,' Howe said, 'staff will be permitted in future to belong only to a departmental staff association approved by their director.'[16] In recognition of these changes (though later the Government was to insist that it related solely to the removal of the employment protection provisions) staff who elected to stay at GCHQ – if they remained in their traditional unions, they were told, they would be transferred to another part of the Civil Service – were each to receive a payment of £1000. Even as Howe spoke, letters were released to all the estimated 7000 GCHQ staff. Included with each letter was a copy of a general management notice, GN 100/84, which spelt out in detail the reasons for the Government's move:

> Ministers believe that those engaged in this kind of work should not come within the ambit of legislation which could lead, for example, to details of GCHQ's operations being discussed before an industrial tribunal. . . . Ministers have also decided that organisations involved in vital intelligence work should be freed as far as possible from the risk of industrial disruption. . . . In future, disciplinary action may be taken against anyone involved in industrial action.

The circular to staff was also a good deal clearer than Howe had been in the House of Commons about what would happen to those staff who refused to sign away their rights under the law: 'Any staff refusing to complete the option form or who, after electing to leave GCHQ, refuse to accept an alternative posting will have their employment terminated from a date to be determined by the director.' There it was: leave your union or take an alternative job elsewhere (if there was one available), or else – the sack.

Shocked, astonished, the unions were appalled that trade unionism could be forbidden so easily; but at the same time they were confident that the case against the ban was so obvious, so right, that the prospect was good of reversing the decision. 'First of all you reason,' said Murray, for whom the GCHQ ban was an important contributory factor in his decision, announced five months later, to resign the TUC general secretaryship, 'you argue, you try and persuade them to change their minds. Surely even Mrs Thatcher can change her mind when she's patently wrong.'[17] For Murray and the Civil Service unions, acting in concert, this was the strategy; in the light of the new mood of realism, they pursued it with vigour and intelligence.

Within weeks, the strategy was shattered. Despite indications to the contrary from Sir Robert Armstrong, Cabinet Secretary, which they were to bitterly regret having swallowed, Murray and the Civil Service union general secretaries had to accept the inevitable: the Prime Minister's wholesale rejection of their line, which included what was a ground-breaking deal for the public sector guaranteeing no disruption at GCHQ through industrial action. It was Mrs Thatcher's insistence, which seemed to grow firmer as the unions offered more and promised more, that the union ban would stand. Murray could barely believe it: 'We have been trying to find out, albeit in a limited area, whether we can build with the Government some relationship of trust and confidence. All that has now been called into question.'[18]

Within a month, the tone had hardened, and the unions had, by withdrawing from the National Economic Development Council, emphasised the gulf which now existed between themselves and the Government. 'What do you expect to happen?' Murray asked. 'That you lie on your back and have your tummy tickled? This is what happens when reasonable men are kicked in the teeth.' Murray had expected that the Government would move to the centre to meet him; the trek back to the unions' previous position looked all the harder after Mrs Thatcher's rejection of the unions' case – particularly so since her decision did not alter the basic premise of the new realism, the change signalled by the 1983 election.

By March, more than 90 per cent of GCHQ staff had been forced from their unions, leaving little more than a handful to fight on, to tour the union conferences, to be buoyed up and swept down as the legal action brought by the unions washed in their favour, and then against them. Larry Smith, then the TGWU's executive officer, was brutal: 'New realism was dead and buried before last Christmas when Maggie Thatcher took secret decisions to ban unions at GCHQ, to persevere with anti-trade union laws, and to take on the miners.'[19]

New Realism Discredited, and Reclaimed: The Miners' Strike

They sang 'Here we go, here we go' as they came out of the pits in March 1984. Even as the Nottinghamshire miners began to voice doubts about being out without a ballot, even as the police convoys began to roll up the M1, even as the first lorry drivers were being approached to shake free the rusty rhetorical shackles of solidarity and instead to keep the coal trucks moving, everything seemed possible to the miners. The strike had a tragic inevitability, as John Lloyd, then Industrial Editor of the *Financial Times*, and the strike's best reporter, put it with startling pertinence on the day it ended:

> It has neatly paralleled the seasons: the surging arrogance of spring, and 'here we go'; the long glorious summer of bathing in sun and impending victory on the undisturbed picket lines; the darkening autumn, when the chill of unspoken defeat gripped stronger with every returning miner; the icy certainty of winter

> collapse, frozen in a rejectionist posture, unable to break back to the time when what had been contemptuously rejected was now desperately sought to touch the ending with 'honour'. That is all that has been neat about it. It has been messy and contradictory, and its ending is too: it has been at once farcical and momentous, cruel and noble in the same minute. As the labour movement's self-appointed guards drag themselves back, finally, from the mouth of the guns, Labour rises in the polls. Revolutionary socialism's set-piece, post-war engagement ends with coffee for the TUC at Number 10.[20]

Even though the seeds of the strike's own failure were there from the start, from the moment the NUM executive gave sanction for area-by-area stoppages to build up in form if not in name a national strike, the NUM's action might still have created a resurgence. The strike might still have been both the vehicle and the inspiration for the battered UK unions (or rather their activists) to draw together and say: *This is it. We matter. And we're going to show you how.*

That the miners would not succeed was clear when Nottinghamshire split open. That the public would not back them was clear from the first opinion polls a few weeks later, and it became clearer as the raw violence of the picket lines and in the pit villages fused parts of the mining communities and fissured others, all the while simply repelling the public, whatever or whoever the cause of the violence might be. That trade unionists, faced with the choice, would not back the miners either, was also detectable from early on.

Sitting outside Bolsover pit in Derbyshire early in the strike, while a few men – but not many – were working inside, local miners' officials, squatting on their heels in the sun, seemed not to notice the coal-laden trucks grinding out of the pit a few feet from them, crossing the road, and then mixing the fresh coal just hauled to the surface with poorer stocks, which had been standing in the open for some months, to make an acceptable blend for the Trent Valley power stations. Eventually, they were asked why they were not trying to stop the lorries breaking their strike. With the quiet, patient look of men explaining the obvious to someone too stupid to see it, they said they had tried, at first. But the drivers had said to them: 'Okay. I won't cross your picket line. But if I don't, when I go back to the firm, I may well get the sack. If I do, then they'll take on another driver. He'll come along. You may ask him, too. He may decide not to cross the line. And he may get the sack. And so it'll go on – until at some point, you get someone who says no, I won't do it. I'm going to cross the line. And if he does, then what's happened? The coal's getting moved. You're still on strike – but eventually, you'll go back to work. And we've lost our jobs. So no – we've got to cross the picket.' For the miners at Bolsover, that seemed at the time unanswerable. It remained so throughout the strike; the only difference was that the gap between theory and practice opened wider. As with much of the strike, TV footage conveyed it most starkly: lorry drivers thundering through Welsh miners' picket lines immediately after film of their own union leaders yet again pledging total support for the NUM.

For Scargill, and for those union leaders who were of his view (though none could match his expression of it, nor his intensity), the strike constituted a serious, revolutionary challenge, in which the micro-economic issue of pit closures was fused with the macro-economic – political and moral too – issue of ousting the Government. The vehicle of the challenge was the hard militancy of the Labour movement's crack troops. But they were never sufficiently united. Not just in Nottinghamshire, either; one miner in the Selby superpit in Yorkshire, for example, vilified his pit union leadership for being too militant – but he himself took an exactly similar line. He went picketing, but had voted Conservative in the 1983 election; he stayed out until the rough and bitter end, but thought early on in the strike that miners in his area were 'losing faith in Mrs Thatcher' over the strike. Such contradictions, constantly posed, never resolved, suggest that the strike was inherently flawed. But by its end, the strike's strategy had failed, and was seen to have failed.

'The failure of Scargillism must have a far-reaching effect,' said John Lyons, general secretary of the EMA. 'It means that the option of militant industrial action to change Government policies must now be closed.' The organised left, from Neil Kinnock, the Labour Co-ordinating Committee and the Communist Party onwards, through to such groups as the Revolutionary Communist Party and Militant, took stock of the strike. Varying degrees of realism ran through their analyses, none more so than Kinnock's scathing speech to the 1985 Party conference in Bournemouth or the TUC's astonishing post-strike summary,[21] presented to the NUM, which infuriated Scargill. Noting that in the period January 1984 to November 1985, which encompassed the strike, its build-up and its immediate aftermath, thirty-five pits had closed or were being reviewed, and that there had been a national fall in manpower in the same period of almost 16 per cent, or just under 29,000 miners, the TUC was almost brutal: 'The choice for the development of the coal industry in the next century is a stark one,' it said. It was a choice between developing new pits and new technology, with the possibility of the industry reverting to a single union, or the 'frightening' prospect of a UK mining industry privatised, declining to negligible proportions or even closed down. Faced with a 'solidly based' breakaway Union of Democratic Minerworkers, born out of the NUM's failure to ballot its members, the TUC concluded: 'A divided miners' union pursuing different policies would make it very difficult, if not impossible, to resist these moves.'

Realism there was – but that was scarcely surprising. The insanity of trying to picket out Ravenscraig, or of picket-line violence, might have seemed to suggest that the much-vaunted new realism had disappeared completely. In fact, beyond the miners' strike, it never went away – a string of little-noticed but vital internal conferences run by the TUC from January 1985 onwards started to flesh out the bones of TUC Strategy. But there was one union which, beyond all others, seemed to recognise fully the industrial, social and political changes which had taken place, and had tried to come to terms with them – the electricians' union EETPU.

5

New Trade Unionism: The EETPU

> 'Traditional union attitudes, based on perpetual strife, are damaging, particularly in industries subjected to rapid technological change. That outdated and counter-productive behaviour is not for us. Our approach is new, different, even unconventional.'[1]

The Electrical, Electronic, Telecommunication and Plumbing Union, Britain's eighth-largest, attracts controversy like a magnet. Is it a supine, bosses' union, collaborating with employers – or is it, in its electricity supply members, one of the country's most industrially powerful unions, capable of wielding immense and socially dislocating strength? Is it predatory, unscrupulous, unassuageably hungry for members – or is it a trail-blazing, progressive, radical force for change in British industrial relations, challenging the orthodoxy of both management and unions? Is it, in short, an appalling corruption of the very principles and practices of British trade unionism – or is it, now, the shape of British unions in the future? It may well be all this, and more besides.

The unique blend of this union, steeped in its past but, more than most unions, embracing the future, drawing together within itself such disparate elements as high-tech microchip workers and the remnants of medieval guilds, should logically render it fundamentally unstable, irredeemably divided. In fact, alone now among British unions (the NUM had seemed so too, at the opposite end of the ideological and political spectrum, until the 1984–5 strike ripped it asunder), the EETPU is wholly coherent, in its philosophy, its practices, its organisation, its politics: no other British union can match the depth or the consistency of its approach. Partly, that is a matter of history: the aftermath of the Communist ballot-rigging scandal in the union in the 1950s saw the new leadership slice through the union to its very bone, cutting out the supporters of the ousted old guard and methodically replacing them with those believing in the new order. The result is a near-total hegemony, unnerving many of its opponents – and they are many and various – by its sheer homogeneity: left-wingers charge it with ideological cloning, so that listening to one EETPU official resembles nothing more closely than listening to another EETPU official. They are right; and it is that constancy which both gives the union strength, sustaining it against all opposition, and leads to its isolation, to its position as the UK labour movement's principal maverick. Its aggressive certainty is rooted in the two crucial elements of its make-up. First, there are its absolute, governing beliefs: it believes in its members, and it believes that its own stance utterly reflects theirs. Second, there is the union's realisation of industrial change, its perception that technological shifts are at once marginalising many other unions and bringing to prominence the EETPU.

Its pragmatism, its voluble rejection of the posture of revolutionary industrial militancy, ensures that it both exemplifies and encapsulates the strands of thinking which came to be known as the TUC's new realism. The EETPU's approach is so interwoven – its philosophy of trade unionism, for instance, both completely informs its attitude towards other trade unions and stems from them; its political stance both springs from the nature of its membership and consistently reinforces it – that to separate it is to reduce it. But for descriptive purposes, it can be seen to have a number of dominant elements.

EETPU Philosophy

'The EETPU is different, and proud of it,' says Eric Hammond, the union's general secretary since 1984.[2] 'If unions are to meet the challenge of the future, they must abandon the rigidities of the past, be ready to change, and to opt for genuine partnership.'[3] More than most unions, the EETPU has tried to do so, learning all the lessons of unemployment and the change in employment, of the shifting pattern of work and of employees, of Labour's shattering electoral defeat in 1983. And it has come to the wrong conclusions, according to its critics. The EETPU thinks otherwise.

Under both Hammond and his predecessor, Frank (now Lord) Chapple, the EETPU has gone back to basics, examining why UK employees should want to belong to a trade union – and why a majority of them do not. The electricians have taken a long, hard look at non-unionism, everywhere on the rise in Britain, and have actively tried to do something to counter it. Many unions have ambitions and make attempts to organise in the non-union sector, but few are achieving any real successes. The EETPU is vigorously part of such efforts – mounting in the high-tech areas of Scotland's central lowlands a lengthy and traditional recruitment campaign, racing round carparks pushing leaflets under windscreen wipers, holding hotel meetings, placing advertisements in the local press. 'We're running a marathon here,' says Bob Eadie, the union's officer organising it.

But the EETPU has gone beyond that, as well. Again, alone among UK unions, it has made a quantum leap in union thinking by aiming its bid for members at *employers* rather than their employees: the more responsibly it can conduct itself, the theory goes, the greater distance it can put between itself and other unions, the more employers will be attracted towards it. Instead of painstakingly recruiting ones and twos in a factory, a handful here and there, why not try to draw into membership the entire workforce of the factory by persuading the employer of the value of having the EETPU as a part of his operation? Says Hammond:

> We co-operate readily with fair employers. They and our members alike gain immensely from the enlightened self-interest involved in doing so and from the presence of our genuinely representative, independent and trustworthy organisation at their workplace. Many managements have good cause to be grateful for our efficiency, expertise and effort. We provide work study, productivity, job evaluation and training services. Our organisation is equipped to help meet the critical needs of Britain's growth industries.[4]

A strong pitch; but in its organisation, its services to members, and in the deals it signs, the EETPU's claim is that it can back it up.

To sell itself to employers, the union launched in July 1984 what is probably one of the most extraordinary documents ever published by a British trade union. Called 'The Union for Your Future', the EETPU's glossy, fourteen-page prospectus – it was nothing short of that – was mailed to 500 employers to convince them of the union's value. Bearing a cover illustrated with silicon chips, it included photographs of the union's French-château-styled training college at

Esher and of its new robot at its high-tech training centre at Cudham in Kent, and a message from both Chapple and Hammond setting out the theory of the EETPU's new unionism. In support were scattered comments from employers and Government ministers, including endorsements from Tom King, then employment secretary, from Kenneth Baker, then technology minister, and this from Sir Walter Marshall, chairman of the Central Electricity Generating Board: 'Your union is a haven of commonsense and rational thought.'[5]

They were not the only ones. Just three months after the defeat of the miners, in which he played a key role, Peter Walker, the energy secretary, visited and warmly approved the Cudham training centre, meeting there twelve Chinese students whom the EETPU were training in electronics skills – a first for a UK union. Walker was following in the footsteps of Norman Tebbit, at that time the industry secretary, who had opened the centre, praising the EETPU's 'progressive approach', and prompting the irrepressible Hammond, a man of some sly wit, to say of the supposed mellowing of Tebbit as the hard man of the Conservative Party: 'Some of our colleagues felt that having you here would be a clear signal to the world of us softening our attitudes.' Kenneth Clarke, the employment minister, told a Conservative conference in December 1985:

> Look at the benefits which membership of the EETPU has brought, not only in terms of job security, but also in the way in which private health care has been negotiated for members of the union at prices they can afford. This, to me, is what good trade unionism should be about – improving the conditions and prospects of ordinary trade unionists and concentrating on the issues that affect them and their families every day.[6]

That might be seen as clear evidence for critics of the union's collaboration with the enemy. Hammond does not see it that way; he distances the union from those who 'retain a belief in the old-style class struggle, and reject co-operation with management in favour of continuing conflict'.

There is a design behind all the EETPU's otherwise apparently deliberately provocative moves. As a major energy union, the EETPU believes it is fully justified in having a relationship with Walker; Tebbit's own department provided £95,000 towards the centre he was opening. But provocation is intended, too: 'I was advised by my father never to strike the first blow,' says Hammond. But the union does like to get its retaliation in first: 'We do respond in a fairly robust way. When you are in a minority, that's probably the only way you're going to have any effect. You can't sit quietly and argue rationally.'[7] EETPU leaders feed off opposition, they perform well when faced with it: 'I do enjoy it, it gees me up,' Hammond says. 'The blood rises once they start on me.'[8] Sometimes, they just cannot resist it: Hammond in 1984 was the first trade union leader to hold a fringe meeting at a CBI conference, as part of the union's strategy of selling itself to employers, and he threw out there the idea of the union applying for membership of the CBI. Partly a joke, partly serious, Hammond appalled the TUC by pressing the idea further publicly, eventually drawing from Kenneth Edwards, the CBI's deputy-director general, a thin-lipped response that the CBI was not the 'right sort' of organisation to represent trade unions.

Overtly aggressive tactics from the union may well impress its members, and even obtain it a few more. 'I must admit, though,' says one of Hammond's TUC General Council colleagues privately, 'that if you talk to most ordinary Labour voters they say things that are uncannily similar to those said by Eric.'[9] But such tactics are not without their cost. Much of the union's argument is lost precisely because of the opposition the union engenders, precisely because what is being said is coming from the EETPU. One senior official of the union acknowledges: 'We do so much damage to our case before we even speak. They don't listen to us; they just vote against us because we're the EETPU.' That reaction to the EETPU stems partly from its near-arrogant isolationism – 'I'm elected by our people,' says another senior lay official, 'and I serve our people, and sod the rest of them' – and partly from the EETPU's tactic of trumpeting developments, like signing single-union deals, which are widespread among other unions, but about which they would rather keep quiet.

Linked to the union's outspokenness is its thoroughgoing populism, its rooted belief in a sustaining symbiosis between the union's leadership and its members. Membership power is a key concept for the union. Hammond says: 'Our union is based on the postal votes of individual members. They vote directly for the executive council, and for the general secretary, who stands for election every five years – not elected for life. They vote on whether or not to take industrial action. We're fully accountable to them.' Advocacy of the postal ballot, of the collected counsel of individual members, is the test by which other unions stand or fall. The activist layer of most unions' representative pyramidal democracy is dismissed; Hammond asks of other unions: 'How can they respond to or reflect their members' interests when their affairs are conducted by leaders and committees accountable only to a thin stratum of activists?' He says: 'In many trade unions policies are decided by conferences and committees rather than by a majority of members. That is based on the idea that readers of the *Sun* and the *Mirror* can't be trusted.'[10]

Blended with that populism, stemming from it, and governing the union, is its pragmatism. Take youth unemployment; the subject of genuine anguish for many current union leaders, many of whom felt it personally earlier in their lives, it is something about which most unions can in practice do little. The EETPU thought differently. Apprenticeships in electrical contracting were falling rapidly in the early 1980s as the recession began to bite. The union could have capitalised on that, pushing up wage rates based on labour scarcity. Instead, it took a longer – and more pragmatic – view. In 1982, it negotiated with the Electrical Contractors' Association a remarkable agreement which reconstituted training in the industry. As part of a whole package, the links between apprentice rates and those of a skilled electrician were broken; the rates for trainees under the new system were roughly two-thirds of those applicable under the old apprentice scheme. As a result of the package, the number of apprentices shot up: from 900-odd in 1982, with the prospect of virtually none the following year, to 2637 in the first year of the new deal. There was outcry from the left in the unions about wage-cutting, but Hammond, who had as a national official negotiated the deal, says now: 'Colleagues in other trade unions who criticise us will have a shrinking number of apprentices, and they will mouth hypocritical phrases and cry crocodile tears about the kids who are not getting trained. We did something about it; the only thing we could do.' In particular, its pragmatism permeates its attitude towards technological change. Some unions have tried to resist it; not so the EETPU. 'My union is bound to go where new technology leads us,' Hammond says. 'New technology is vital to Britain's industrial survival.' It is an approach that is clearly attractive to employers, and to employees, since it promises the one co-operation rather than conflict over technical change, and the other enhanced skills and better job prospects.

The new unionism, then, as the EETPU defines it, is strong,

populist, co-operative; forward-looking, flexible, technologically based; unashamedly pragmatic. But for the electricians, it does not just exist as theory, as a strategy; the whole point is to put it into practice.

EETPU Membership

The EETPU draws much of its philosophy from what its leaders identify as the characteristics of electricians as an industrial breed: individualistic, skilled, flexible, argumentative, mobile, entrepreneurial, *different*. Within that framework, its membership straddles a number of boundaries, with large sections in the general engineering industry, in electrical contracting and in electricity supply. The majority of its members are skilled workers, with substantial numbers as technicians or in clerical and professional work.

The skill base of the union's membership is apparent. Much of its members' work is in maintenance, and increasing use of electronics means electricians are likely to remain in demand, as one official from one of the EETPU's competitor unions rather ruefully acknowledges: 'In most workplaces there is the increasing introduction of electronics technology in ordinary jobs – all of which needs maintenance people. That is the EETPU's main growth area.' But even though demand for their skills may give electricians greater job security than many manual workers, even those with skills, electricians' skills are often allied to particular technical forms; when those forms change, jobs can be under threat, no matter how skilled the employee.

To counter this, the union in 1980 began a technical training programme which EETPU leaders now claim is the most advanced trade union training facility in Europe. Certainly in the UK it has no rivals. Not just among unions, either: since its founding, more than 700 companies had by the end of 1985 made use of the union's high-tech training programme, based at Cudham Hall – including GEC, Kelloggs, British Rail, the CEGB, Goodyear, the Ministry of Defence, GKN, Thames Water, the LEB, Birds Eye, Wiggins Teape, British Aerospace and Yorkshire Television. Why? Why do profitable, efficient companies turn to a union for training? Dave Rogers, the EETPU's head of technical training, says: 'When we first started, we didn't think that the big companies would use us. We thought they would have their own resources.' They were wrong: companies use the EETPU's training because it is cheaper, because of its quality, and because of the breadth of skills offered – at Cudham, at the union's nine regional centres, and even by its mobile training unit, putting facilities at the factory door.

It works, too. An internal survey of those passing through Cudham found that of those who had been unemployed before they went on the course, more than half found jobs after it. The objective of job security was achieved for others: 93 per cent remained with their employers, though often doing different work; 15 per cent were upgraded after taking the course.[11] 'As a direct result of Cudham Hall teaching and my learning I have now, after a six-month trial period, secured myself full-time employment as an electrical engineer,' said one EETPU member from Sheffield. 'It pays very handsomely, and it's great to be working again.'[12] 'I learnt more about electronics in one week at Cudham Hall than in four years' technical college,' said another, from Peterborough. And a member from Hereford said: 'I cannot express in words the invaluable service the EETPU training course has given me and my family . . . my small thank you is to always remain a member of the EETPU.'[13]

Belatedly, other unions have started to follow suit: in February 1986 the engineering workers' union started to train a small number of members in robotics and computer-controlled machinery at residential centres in London and Nottingham.

But the EETPU does not just concentrate on its members' working lives. As well as bargaining on their pay and conditions, unions have always provided a range of services for their members. Traditionally, these have been mainly in areas like death or sickness benefit. In January 1986 the EETPU launched a unique, comprehensive package of financial benefits providing advantageous rates on services ranging from unit trusts to vehicle breakdown and recovery. Eric Hammond says the move is 'breaking entirely new ground for the British trade union movement. Once again we are in the vanguard of change.' Negotiated by Alan Pickering, the EETPU's deputy research head, the services offered include a special introduction to the Halifax Building Society for mortgages, with some fixed-price legal conveyancing; 20 per cent discount on Cornhill house insurance; special price membership of Octagon, a leading non-AA/RAC car breakdown service; preferential savings rates with the Bradford and Bingley Building Society; a 2 per cent bonus issue of units with M&G, Britain's largest unit trust group; a new policy with Provident Mutual providing for buy-outs when members leave occupational pension schemes; employer insurance for members who set up in their own businesses; and share advice using a firm of London stockbrokers.

With the prospect of controlled access to a range of skilled, well-paid employees, the companies involved are enthusiastic. Bob Clarke, managing director of Octagon Recovery, says: 'The union appears to be doing something for their members, as opposed to engaging in political infighting.' Richard Coles, Halifax regional operations controller in London, explains: 'It will be an encouragement to union members to approach building societies if they have previously been afraid to do so.' Says Christopher Reading, Provident Mutual's controller of individual pensions: 'It's a logical step for a union to recommend a package like this to their members.' Jokingly, Hammond talks of representing members from the cradle to the grave; the union is aware that improved services are unlikely by themselves to win members for the union. But they will help to keep them; and that is a clear advantage in a trade union environment where competition for members is now fierce.

EETPU Organisation

The EETPU's key selling-point in negotiating with financial services companies for preferential rates for its members was its computerised central membership register. Given the union's insistence on the ballot-based primacy of its membership in decision-making, the computer is now vital for the union's whole organisation – 'the bedrock of our democracy', Frank Chapple called it. The Government's requirement in the 1984 Trade Union Act for centralised membership lists is forcing many unions to come to terms with computer technology, but it is unlikely that many will quickly rival the two leaders in the field – Tass, the engineering union, and the electricians. The EETPU's £302,000 Honeywell DPS7 system holds detailed records of all the union's members – job, employer, branch, home and work addresses, payments and union history. One of its most important tasks is now communication, sending the union's journal *Contact* to members' homes six times a year, and providing the union with a powerful weapon, if necessary: when the EETPU successfully fought against the breakaway of its Fleet Street branch to join Sogat, EETPU officials were confident that they could always win in the end because they had the technical ability, unmatched even by the branch itself, to put their case into the homes of every branch member every day, if necessary. The union saves £50,000 a year by computer pre-sorting its automatically addressed membership mail into postcode areas, and it has cut down its subscription arrears dramatically. It is not cheap: according to its 1984 accounts, computer maintenance and leasing cost the union £72,528, though officials do not begrudge a penny.

Financially, the EETPU in 1984 had a total net worth of just over £11.3 million – almost £29 per member. Much of that, about £3.73 million, was in fixed assets, mainly property. A further £6.5 million was held in equities – a substantial proportion in Government stock, but including 25,000 shares in Allied Lyons, 21,000 in Plessey, 20,000 each in Glaxo and Commercial Union, 17,000 in TI, 13,500 in ICI and 7200 in Thorn-EMI.[14] Since December 1985, the union has boosted its finances by applying to the Government for money to fund its own postal ballots, after its members had defied the then TUC policy and voted 9–1 in favour. Computerisation has helped reduce the burdens on shop stewards (the union has around one for every twenty-seven members, roughly twice the number in many other unions) of chasing overdue subscriptions.

Organisationally, the union has three separate, though related, structures – constitutional, with branches feeding through the union's biennial delegate conference (advisory, rather than policy-making) to the full-time executive; industrial, with stewards in each industry covered by the union sending delegates to area and then national industrial conferences, which are linked to national industrial officers and their committees, and then to the executive; and political, with regional political conferences electing annual Labour Party delegates and members of the national political advisory committee, which sponsors MPs and reports to the executive.

Within these interrelated structures, the executive is clearly the key body. Widely seen outside the union as monolithic and impenetrable, the fifteen-strong executive (thirteen divisional members – ten electrical, three plumbing – the plumbing secretary and the general secretary) is not quite that – though at the beginning of 1986, with only two exceptions, it was solidly right-wing. Critics of the union suggest that real power lies elsewhere; a former employee writes: 'It became very obvious after only a few days spent working in the EETPU head office that the union was run by a tight-knit group of leaders, and that this group was not the ostensible ruling body of the EETPU, namely, the executive council.'[15] Union officials testify privately that, under Chapple especially, the 'magic circle' of key associates were the real power in the union; those not in the chosen few rarely saw Chapple, let alone had much influence upon him, or upon the union's direction.

As in most unions, the general secretary wields considerable power. This is all the more true in the EETPU, which although it makes a virtue of ballot-box democracy does not, unlike the AUEW, elect its officials. Alone among the appointed officers, the general secretary is elected, which gives him an authority unique in the union. Hammond, elected in 1982, won by a substantial margin, polling 73,506 votes (55.3 per cent of those voting) against the left's candidate, John Aitken (32,436 votes; 24.4 per cent) and the centrist, Roy Sanderson (26,945; 20.3 per cent).

Chapple was an extraordinary leader. Rough, charismatic, belligerent and autocratic, he was scathing about almost everybody. Clive Jenkins, of ASTMS, was a 'pipsqueak', Neil Kinnock a 'political eunuch'; David Basnett, former general secretary of GMBATU, was 'so often weak and vacillating', Tony Benn a 'political knave and double-dealer'. Special mention for Arthur Scargill: a 'big-mouth and a raging egomaniac'.[16] With quotes like that, Chapple was a natural for the newspapers; his frequent signed columns, mostly in the popular press, and often precisely timed to rub salt into a wound particularly gaping at the time, launched him with his retirement into a permanent column with the *Daily Mail*.

Chapple was fuelled by his anti-Communism, and especially by the union's own ballot-rigging scandal. Hammond, though a hard right-winger and Chapple's favoured son to succeed him ('If you think I'm right-wing,' Chapple remarked gleefully, 'wait until you see Eric'), is less gripped by the CP. No Chapple clone, Hammond is both more open than Chapple – 'Eric will ring you up,' says one of his lay officials, 'and say there might be a problem: why not do this? Frank would ring up, occasionally, and shout what the hell have you done down there? Get it changed' – and more opaque, too: 'Frank you could hear coming,' another EETPU insider says; 'Eric sneaks up on you.' Or as one TUC General Council member put it: 'Eric says the same things as Frank – but he says them with a smile.' Hammond can be disarming, but he can roar with the best of them, too. To the appalled disquiet of left-wing delegations, basking warmly in the aftermath of Chapple's departure, Hammond hit the 1983 TUC Congress with a brutal attack on 'terrorists, lesbians and other queer people' in London Labour Parties, earning himself a rebuke from then general secretary Len Murray for his 'offensive' statements.[17]

Hammond looks every inch a businessman, with a copy of the *Financial Times* on the back seat of his car, a carphone in the front. Born in Gravesend, north Kent, in 1929, the son of a paper-mill worker, Hammond still lives in neighbouring Northfleet. Joining the electricians' union as an apprentice in 1945 on his return from evacuation in Newfoundland, Hammond became a shop steward and married in 1953. He was and is very pro-Labour, having no truck, unlike Chapple, with the SDP. Five years a local councillor, he was elected to the EETPU executive in 1963 with left-wing support; he was the anti-establishment candidate. A do-it-yourself enthusiast, photographer and voracious reader, Hammond was seen by other executive members at first as rather quiet and ordinary, who got on with carrying out his allotted tasks. But his stature grew until it became clear that Chapple wished to see the mantle of leadership fall to him. Since taking over, he has cast aside Chapple's shadow – no mean feat – partly by out-Franking even Frank, but partly by winning the confidence of the executive, by leaving officers to carry out their negotiations alone, by revitalising and refurbishing the divisional offices, by laying strong emphasis on technological change, and by grasping the range of issues in which the EETPU is involved at once vigorously and intellectually. Publicity helped him to forge a widely recognisable identity. To one of his criticisms of the TUC, Norman Willis – no mean wit himself – replied: 'This is just Eric being Eric.' No one was in any doubt what he meant.

EETPU Politics

'We're not a moderate union,' says one senior EETPU official, with pride and relish. 'We're a *right-wing* union!' The EETPU is the arch-bastion of the trade union and Labour Party right, and fights its corner hard. But it also claims to be almost apolitical: 'We reject the use of unions to undermine democratically elected governments or as debating societies for fringe political agitators.'[18] What that may mean in practice is that the union rejects such tactics where they are used *by the left*; in its own terms, its politics are central. 'The EETPU', writes an ex-employee, 'is an intensely political trade union.'[19] Its political approach is remarkably consistent ('political activity on the right of the Labour Party is, in fact, the *sine qua non* for a successful career as an official of the EETPU'),[20] and operates both within the union and without.

Internal

Left-wingers in the EETPU have a tough time of it. Compared with the dominant right wing now in control of the union, there are not many of them: the broad left meetings at the union's conference attract only a handful of conference delegates (though the meetings themselves are quite full; a substantial part of the audience are right-wing union officials, smiling genially and taking notes). But that is hardly surprising; since the early 1960s, the left in the union has at best been isolated, more often rooted out. Though its immediate, practical influence is lessening, the dominant internal political factor is still the court battles of twenty-five years ago, which saw the union's corrupt, Communist leadership finally ripped from power.[21] Even at his retirement, it was Chapple's key reference: 'An incomparable turning-point for me'. The long, lonely struggle for power in the union in the 1950s, led by Les Cannon, Chapple's predecessor, in which Chapple played a part, eventually ended up in a complex, forty-two-day High Court action, costing more than £90,000, which found guilty of fraudulent ballot-rigging five senior officials of the union, including its president, Frank Foulkes, and its general secretary, Frank Haxell. Despite the court findings, the Communist leadership (apart from Haxell, deposed by the court case) tried to hang on, but were almost completely ousted in the next executive elections.

The right in the union then set about root and branch reform. Its assault on the left was so thorough, so extensive as to alter the entire complexion of the union: its opponents, in retreat, charged it with inexorable centralisation, of silencing all opposition, of in effect remoulding the union into a right-wing mirror-image of its old Communist days. Many left-wingers underwent wholesale conversions (Chapple and Cannon had both been Communists themselves); the list of officials now in senior positions in the union who used to be pillars of the left is extraordinarily extensive. In particular, the left repeatedly tried to repeal the ban on members of the Communist Party holding office in the union, instituted after a 3–1 ballot vote in October 1964. 'The EETPU's attitude towards political and industrial affairs generally is dictated by an intense anti-communist approach, which, if it was equalled throughout the movement in Britain, would put McCarthyism in the shade,' according to a group of Communist members in the union.[22] 'Always a major consideration of the executive council's majority is – how to keep the left down?' Rules-revision conferences take place in the EETPU every six years (the next is scheduled for 1989); in 1983, when ending the ban was last debated, the rule embodying it was overwhelmingly supported.

Left-wingers in the union have gathered around a number of publications over the years – *Flashlight*, *Beacon*, *Rank and File Contact*, *Progressive Electricians' Bulletin*. The Flashlight group, a mixture of left Labour and Communist members, is the most significant of them, arguing against most aspects of current EETPU policy but particularly vociferous on the strike-free deals – 'a new dimension to the old-fashioned compromises and sell-outs'.[23] Flashlight argues for the EETPU to be shunned, as its pre-1985 Labour Party conference issue suggested: 'Previous congresses have found the EETPU in isolation, because of its divisive role. We urge that this position be sustained in the most emphatic way at this 1985 conference.'[24]

Hammond puts the 100-odd who attend the conference broad-left meetings together with the 332 members who attended the branch meetings putting forward at the 1983 conference the raft of key rule amendments, including ending the Communist ban, against his own vote in the previous year's general-secretaryship election. Yet John Aitken, a *Daily Mail* electrician and leading EETPU left-winger, who stood against Hammond, included an end to the Communist ban as part of his election manifesto – and secured almost a quarter of the available votes. The left may be a rump in the EETPU, but it is still not without its strength. One index of that is the attention it is given by the union's leadership: for example, when the *Financial Times* reported the formation in December 1985 of a new left grouping to encompass all the left's internal groups (though the new group was itself Militant-dominated), union officials telephoned industrial correspondents other than the reporter who wrote the article, asking them if they knew who its sources were, and who had attended the group's founding meeting in Liverpool.

The sixty-five-odd founders in an upper room in the polytechnic students' union in the city were genuinely wary of their names becoming known, for fear of retaliatory action against them by the union. The EETPU has a chequered though detailed history of moving against internal opposition, particularly by the closure or amalgamation of dissident branches.[25] The attitude behind such action is still there, an inevitable consequence of rejecting the activist level in favour of the membership; one senior official tells of finally visiting a nominally 1000-strong branch, after lengthy entreaty, to be greeted there by vitriolic attacks from just seven people – 'the sort of people you wouldn't sit next to on a bus'. Militant accuses the EETPU leadership of a 'refusal to accept any kind of class perspective' as the key to understanding postal ballots and strike-free deals;[26] this reveals the scale of the continuing internal divisions within the union over its strategy and approach, for the EETPU's leadership argue for the agreements precisely in terms of class.

External

John Spellar, the EETPU's cherubic, bearded political officer and head of research, clearly could not resist it at the 1985 Labour Party conference in Bournemouth. Sharply dressed Derek Hatton, Liverpool's Militant city council deputy leader, had been prominent at the conference, as Militant was routed by Neil Kinnock. Opening his speech on one man, one vote, Spellar could not miss the opportunity: 'John Spellar, EETPU,' he began, holding his lapels, 'wearing Derek Hatton's suit.' Spellar, briefly Labour MP for Birmingham Northfield, and contesting it again at the next election, is a key figure in the union's external and internal political structures. Conspiratorial, engaging, he is held in some awe in the union: 'How well *do* you know John?' people ask. His cheerful aggression and tireless work is characteristic of the union's political activity. 'During the 15 months I was employed in the research department,' a former subordinate writes, 'I was approached no less than four times by the persistent head of research who wanted me to be active in the Brighton Labour party. Eventually, without my permission, he placed me on the Brighton Kemptown general management committee of the Labour party as a delegate from the EETPU general office branch – which never meets. Every other research officer was subject to the same pressure.'[27]

Despite suspicions, that activity is wholly centred on the Labour Party. Chapple signed the original 1981 declaration of support for the Council of Social Democracy, which eventually transformed itself into the SDP, but that was in large part due to his long-standing friendship with John Grant, a former *Daily Express* industrial correspondent, Labour MP and employment minister who left the Party in 1981 for the Social Democrats. Grant is now the union's head of communications, but the SDP presence in the union goes little further than that. Chapple had his own views: 'I probably admire her as much as anyone on my executive,' he said of Mrs Thatcher;[28] on another occasion, he suggested that trade unions 'have to choose between socialism and survival'.[29]

The EETPU has fought hard in the constituency parties for its view, often adopting many of the left's tactics, and leading to charges from left-wingers of packing meetings, acting unfairly. All grist to the EETPU mill; its leaders argue they may have fought hard, but they fight openly. Like the AUEW, the EETPU was one of the few unions in the 1985–6 political fund ballots which linked the vote not just to political representation, but to Labour specifically: 'History has shown that Labour governments have helped trade unions, their members and their families. That is why the EETPU and other trade unions have affiliated to the party. To continue to do so we shall have to maintain our political fund.'[30] Its frankness paid off: in the largest vote in the union's history, a 42 per cent turnout, the result of its ballot, declared in August 1985, was decisive – 140,913 (84 per cent) in favour of retaining the fund, with 26,830 (16 per cent) against. Hammond is insistent that even if suspended from the TUC, the EETPU would resist strongly any similar moves to exclude it from the Labour Party. The union has its differences with Labour – on constitutional matters, on issues such as defence; it may be a thorn in Labour's side, as much as in the TUC's; but, for its part, its allegiance to the party is assured.

EETPU Inter-Union Relations

'We are in a free market for trade unionism,' says Roy Sanderson, the EETPU's national engineering officer. 'It exists. We are not trying to create it.' Certainly, most unions are hungry for members; the EETPU is voracious. 'Pirates', a senior Government industrial relations official calls the union. Eric Hammond is personally no supporter of the closed shop. He prefers to win people to union membership, not press them. Hammond would like to see the market unionism now espoused by the EETPU extended, urging that the TUC's 'Bridlington' rules on inter-union demarcations should be relaxed. Bridlington has created a captive membership, he argues, helping to make unions sloppy, letting leaders take their members for granted. 'Anything which loosens that up, and makes us leaner and sharper, might well be to the good.' Such a 'revolutionary factor in trade unionism' would be 'difficult and chaotic, but it might be good for trade unionism'. Hammond's critics would suggest that what he is arguing for might be good for the EETPU, but not more generally; they see the union as predatory, unprincipled, out for members at any cost.

The EETPU's market drive leads it towards innovation: its unprecedented promotional mission to Japan in October 1984 – 'a little pre-emptive work', according to Hammond; a four-week tour round Japanese companies thinking of investing in the UK, and showing them before they came the sort of agreements the EETPU could give them, before they arrived. It also leads it towards inter-union difficulties – most obviously at News International and at Hitachi, but much more extensively, too: Figure 5.1, based on the most difficult of inter-union problems charted each year in the TUC's annual report, illustrates the extent of the EETPU's involvement in disputes between unions,[31] sometimes as complainant, sometimes complained against. These problems would be vastly amplified if the EETPU were to leave the TUC; the electricians are confident that, freed from Bridlington, they could pick up many more members from employers and employees who would rather

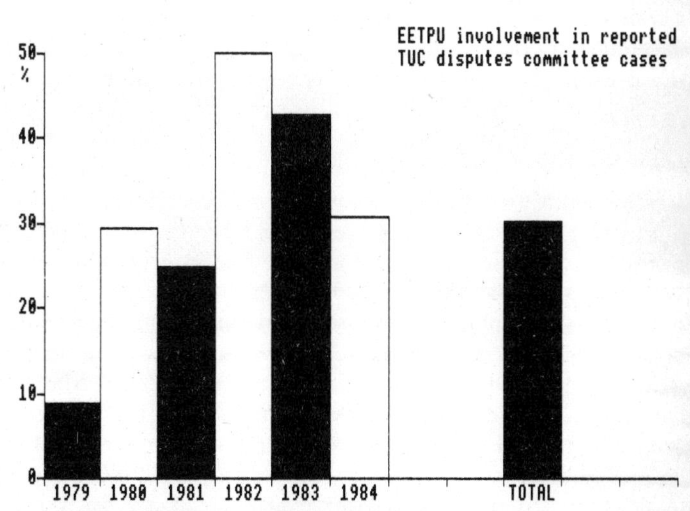

Figure 5.1: EETPU - Inter-union difficulties 1979-84 Source: TUC

work with them – but they also know that many of their members, working often in very small groups, are isolated and vulnerable.

Some in the union's leadership relish the prospect; Hammond is not one of them. He is not looking for 'a lone wolf role, fighting it out with TUC affiliates in 1,001 hand-to-hand combats on shop floors across the country'.[32] But the union has little time for the TUC. 'The trade union movement', says John Grant, 'remains for the most part more inward-looking, defensive and frightened of change than at any time since the 1926 general strike.'[33] Some in the EETPU were openly gleeful about cocking a snook at the TUC in applying for Government ballot money. But, in turn, many in the TUC have little time for the electricians. 'They are very strident,' says Rodney Bickerstaffe, of Nupe, 'almost pushing out their jaw and saying "have a go."'[34] Ken Gill of Tass accuses them of betrayal. Brenda Dean of Sogat sees them as 'scavengers'. They do have friends – John Spellar is a key organiser in the right-wing cross-union pressure group, Mainstream, though in fact the union has alienated some of the right because it has traditionally seemed to prefer isolation, pulling up the drawbridge and settling back in its Kent country house. Even so, Gavin Laird, of the AUEW, calls them a 'progressive union', very much in line with his own. But Jimmy Airlie, the AUEW executive's sole left-winger, disagrees: 'I think the EETPU leadership is an extremist organisation. I think that they would welcome suspension or expulsion.'[35] Even those who would naturally support them have been made unsure. 'I just don't understand what they're doing,' says one prominent engineering union leader. Jack Whyman of the AUEW executive is more figurative: 'You can't apply to join a racing pigeon club and then demand the right to bring a cat in.'[36]

The miners' strike was the most graphic example of the differences – and the connections – between the EETPU and other unions. Scargill's revolutionary stance and the leadership's failure to ballot the union's members set the EETPU against the strike: 'Lions led by donkeys!' Hammond roared at the 1985 Labour conference, to howling derision. The union balloted its members on supporting the miners; the result was an 8–1 vote against. Weeks earlier, at the annual TUC Congress, while the strike was in full swing, Hammond articulated what most knew, what almost all refused to say, and what proved to be entirely correct: that the TUC's promise of physical support for the strike was dishonest, because it was knowingly unrealisable. Hammond's analysis was taken up across virtually the entire political spectrum – but only when the strike was over, as he acidly pointed out to Labour's Bournemouth conference the following year.

The EETPU, through its Nottingham office, began to forge links with the working miners, and eventually with the breakaway Union of Democratic Mineworkers. Fused by a joint commitment to ballot-based democracy, they made manifest the relationship at a joint meeting, ostensibly on energy policy, but with the unwritten agenda of its political dimension too, at Cudham Hall in January 1986. 'It's important', said Hammond, 'that the UDM recognise that they have friends inside the TUC.' Friends they might have, but for how long inside the TUC? Asked over single-union agreements, asked over Government ballot money, asked over the UDM, asked over Wapping, both sides drew back from answering it, and moved to a new rapprochement; it remains an open question.

EETPU: Strike-Free Agreements

The EETPU has championed strike-free deals both as the practical distillation of its new brand of trade unionism and as genuinely offering a solution to many of Britain's industrial problems. As a result, the union has repeatedly been accused of giving up freely the right to strike. Its critics, though, fail to deal adequately with a central point: the EETPU is a highly militant union. Mostly, given its stress on responsible trade unionism, the electricians do not care for that to be widely realised, though they acknowledge it themselves: 'Electricians are a narky bunch,' says a senior official. 'We spend most of our time either sanctioning strikes, or trying to calm them down.'

Left-wingers in the unions were discomposed when Eric Hammond, the arch right-winger, the supreme new realist, announced that the union would ballot its power-station members on strike action if the Government dismissed any GCHQ employees for remaining in or joining a trade union – and the union was confident of a vote in favour. 'This is but a small example of the power of our class,' said the Militant-dominated Broad Left Organising Committee, conveniently forgetting Militant's own constant criticism of the EETPU.[37] By early 1985, secret ballots in the union, taken in line with the Government's 1984 Trade Union Act, were running in favour of industrial action. In June, striking electricians at Vauxhall's Ellesmere Port plant on Merseyside forced the company to concede that they, and not Tass members, should effectively retain control of production-monitoring computer equipment. Over Christmas, ITV electricians taking action forced the independent companies to outlaw casual labour. Each EETPU executive meeting has a host of disputes to consider (not including the repeated local-level flare-ups which never reach national level). Take the meeting of 10 December 1984. The executive's confidential minutes record no less than fourteen disputes for discussion, ranging from Austin Rover to Lucas, from the Port Talbot steel complex to the atomic power station at Dounreay. The following month's minutes add a further eight new disputes, for example at Thorn-EMI, Perkins Engines, Aveling Barford and Plessey.[38] Hardly a no-strike record.

So why strike-free agreements? Unbound by pro-strike, ideological considerations, standing aside from emotion, the EETPU looks at strikes functionally: what are they for? Who do they benefit? What do they achieve? What do they cost? Roy Sanderson is pivotal in this thinking. Calm and rational, Sanderson is like many in the union, a former Communist, quitting the Party twenty-five years ago while he was still a convenor at Lucas. He is a labour movement byword for competence, and for preaching the virtues of the strike-free deals, arguing succinctly, comprehensively and coherently from Cambridge high tables to factory shopfloors, from hostile union conferences to musing circles of industrial relations specialists. To Sanderson, the miners' strike was just the most glaring example of the pointlessness of the strike as a mechanism, making loud noises, but delivering nothing. He says of traditional union attitudes:

> Our approach to industrial relations not only tragically failed the miners but it's not prevented our members slipping further and further down the international league when it comes to pay and security of employment. British unions address every problem in the main with a militant solution. But the track record shows that compared to other unions around the world who adopt a more co-operative, more harmonious attitude, we've done very badly by our members.

Sanderson started to formulate his theories more fully when he carried out in 1979 and 1980 a rough survey of all the strikes involving EETPU members in engineering, the industry for which he has national responsibility. 'What that survey showed was that in a two-year period, our members who'd been on strike were going back to work with either what was offered to them before they came out or so little of a difference as to make the strike an absolute nonsense.' Caught up in a whirling complex of grievance, emotion, hope and fear, strikes are rarely analysed in such a functional manner. But research work bears out Sanderson's empirical theory. Studying four separate disputes, Gennard found that in each there were substantial net losses – losing £107 to gain £25 in one case, £137 to gain £85, £147 to gain £36, and £407 to gain £115.[39] Dow suggests that if employees strike for six months, and win 5 per cent higher wages as a result, it would take them seven or eight years to win back what they had lost, even if the 5 per cent differential were maintained that long. An employer in a corresponding position might lose a year's profits.[40]

Sanderson's conclusion was clear. 'We took the view that if strikes are failing to win members what it is they might deserve, then we should be looking for some alternative to strikes as a means of doing it.' He started from basics, thinking through what causes conflict in industry. 'The fact is that in most of British industry there is still a class system in which the manual worker is at the bottom of the pile, he's the second-class citizen' – worse hours, worse conditions, worse pay, worse benefits. Sanderson became convinced that the way to resolve this potential source of conflict was Japanese-style egalitarianism – single-status. But for employees there was another area of difficulty. Sanderson felt that many British managements were secretive, with information given out only on a need-to-know basis. Possession of information confirmed management separateness, and that seemed to be essential for managing people. He coupled that with his view that 'British workers, no matter how intelligent they are, are never given a chance of a real say in how the company is run.' Some form of genuine industrial democracy was therefore required. From the management's viewpoint, rigid demarcation caused difficulty, too; functional flexibility was the answer, but in Sanderson's scheme it had to be reciprocal – flexibility had to be accompanied by training.

With all those elements in place, Sanderson reasoned, the likelihood of conflict would be greatly reduced. But it could still break out; to resolve it, arbitration seemed the obvious answer. But could binding arbitration, both unions and management ceding final control to a third party, be compatible with collective bargaining, with the exercise of proper union–management functions? Under an arbitration system Sanderson discovered called pendulum arbitration, it seemed as though it could. The strike-free package was born.

6

Strike-Free Agreements: The Package

From the Confederation of British Industry at Eastbourne to the Fabian Society at Blackpool, from Business International in London to the Institute of Personnel Management in Harrogate, from Aston University in Birmingham to the TUC in Brighton – let alone within its own ranks – the EETPU has been proclaiming the word, its vision of the future now being enacted in the present: strike-free agreements. In a sense, its near-religious fervour has paid off – interest in the EETPU deals among managers is startlingly high. At the 1984 CBI conference in Eastbourne, for instance, it was standing-room only to hear Eric Hammond detail the theory of the union's new agreements; no less so a few months earlier, when Roy Sanderson did the same, to considerably less approval, at the TUC Congress in Brighton.

Yet the union acknowledges that its ideas have not been spreading as fast as they would have liked, that companies have not been as quick to seize the opportunity the EETPU believes it is offering. Perhaps that is because companies which have notably rejected the EETPU package deal, such as Thorn-EMI and GEC, do not see it that way; they see the offer as a poisoned chalice, attractive in parts (the provisions making strikes unlikely) but tainted in others (the regular disclosure of detailed commercial information). But what the EETPU is now offering *is* a package, coherent and mutually interdependent. Wyn Bevan, who as the EETPU's executive councillor for Wales and the South West has more of these agreements within his constituency than any other senior official of the union, says:

> Many employers would love for the EETPU to insert clauses into their current agreements bringing about pendulum arbitration or binding conciliation. The answer is – they will not get it. But if an employer wishes to avail himself of pendulum arbitration or any other means of resolving disputes, then he must accept the total package of our agreements with the aim of transforming the relationship with people at work.[1]

Acas, Britain's most widely respected independent industrial relations institution, agrees. In a confidential briefing paper to staff, Acas says: 'In that the EETPU agreements combine a number of elements to create a whole package, the no-strike deals can be seen as unique.'[2]

EETPU leaders no longer like the phrase 'no-strike deal' (though, interestingly, a number of leaders of the union have material on these agreements filed away under precisely that heading). They argue that their agreements do not yield up the 'right' to strike, employees' ability to withdraw their labour. Since their agreements are not legally binding, employees covered by them can, if they wish, break them – they *can* strike. In part, though many in the EETPU feed off criticism, the renaming of these agreements has been a response to the savage reaction they have prompted within the unions, as Sir Pat Lowry, Acas chairman, notes: 'Eric Hammond and his colleagues in the EETPU continue to antagonise their colleagues in other unions, not least by virtue of the so-called "no-strike" agreements which they vigorously espouse.'[3]

Ron Todd, general secretary of the TGWU, says: 'I would never append my signature to an agreement that removed the right of members to withdraw their labour.'[4] His colleague, Larry Smith, TGWU assistant general secretary, says: 'They should be banned by the TUC for giving away the ultimate protection workers possess.'[5] 'Sweetheart deals,' Campbell Christie, general secretary of the Scottish TUC, calls them. Tom Sawyer, of the public employees' union Nupe, told his union's annual conference: 'The only thing you have got to be to sign a no-strike agreement is a bloody fool.' Academics, too: 'The "no-strike" agreement is a brittle concord to sustain even for the most sophisticated managerial repertoires, but without the in-plant innovations . . . together with the solvent of growth upon which much depends, "no-strike" agreements have little chance of being established, let alone sustained.'[6] – though others, more prominent, are less sceptical: 'This co-operation may be the only means of preventing the expansion of non-union employer practices.'[7] Unsurprisingly, the aggressive EETPU does not care: 'There's no opposition among rank-and-file members to this type of agreement,' says Sanderson. 'There might be among activists and leaders and academics and reporters. But there's not among rank and file members, none whatsoever.'

Sanderson may well be right. MORI found more than 60 per cent of both the public and trade unionists to be in favour of strike-free deals, and the industrial communications company EPIC found a growing swell of support among managers and a reasonably high level of approval among trade unionists.[8]

Managers *may* be reluctant to take the plunge and sign a deal with the EETPU, or the AUEW (as at Nissan), or the TGWU (as at Norsk Hydro), because of the radical opportunities that these agreements offer to their workforces, but the climate may be changing. Take Dr James MacFarlane, director-general of the Engineering Employers' Federation, and one of industry's most practical, least idealistic, proponents. Espousing the value of workplace flexibility and single-union provisions, both key features of the strike-free package, Dr MacFarlane says:

> It enables an employer to select a moderate and progressive-minded union with which he can agree to operate from the outset an industrial relations culture embracing all the different aspects . . . that is, employee involvement, harmonisation and the flexibility of labour. To this may be added the benefits of features such as 'no-strike clauses', pendulum arbitration and long-term agreements. At present the single-union agreement is probably only generally obtainable in 'greenfield' factories. But, assuming the promised advantages materialise, it could in time exercise a profound effect on British industrial relations culture.[9]

MacFarlane identifies the elements which, woven together, form the strike-free package, pursued most prominently by the EETPU. Those elements are far from new, as many of the EETPU's critics have vigorously pointed out. As Acas notes: 'There are other agreements, both modern and long-standing, containing similar provisions to some of those found in the EETPU deals.'[10] Lord McCarthy, the seasoned industrial relations expert, sees their roots deep in long-standing practice: 'In some ways, these agreements have a very long tradition in certain parts of industry.'[11] Even so, the package has been widely misinterpreted. In particular, none of the deals signed by the beginning of 1986 carried legal enforceability (though Rupert Murdoch repeatedly and incorrectly cited them as legally binding deals during his dispute with the print unions over his new plant at Wapping). Roy Sanderson is unconvinced of the applicability of legal enforcement to the strike-free package: 'It would, in my opinion, turn industrial relations in this country from bad to worse, because it's the approach of consent and agreement that really ensures any long-lasting reform of our system. It would turn our system into a quagmire.'

A key misunderstanding, too, has been to see the elements which make up the strike-free package as wholly Japanese in their origin. They are not that, even though Sanderson, their principal architect, is an admirer of Japanese employee-relations practices (and a regular visitor to Japan, too; one senior union official said after visiting Japan himself that Sanderson was the only British union official apart from Arthur Scargill of whom the Japanese had ever heard). He says: 'There was certainly no attempt to copy Japanese industrial practice. The aim at the outset was to identify British industrial relations problems and to form British solutions to them. Now it's true that the final package did coincide quite a bit with what happens in Japan. But we didn't set out to import and to graft on a Japanese industrial relations package. That was not our intention.' Many of the strike-free deals *have* been signed with Japanese companies, but other owners are American, Norwegian – even British. Most Japanese companies in the UK do not feature them. Many Japanese companies operating in Britain are non-union: Jetro estimates that about 38 per cent of Japanese subsidiaries in the EEC are non-union, while 44 per cent have some form of in-house, company union – roughly comparable to the position in Japan itself.[12] Some key Japanese employment practices – in particular the idea of 'lifetime' employment (though in fact this only covers a core of Japanese workers) – have not in the main been translated to Europe, for primarily cultural reasons – as Jetro suggests in a further survey, referring to 'local' European employees:

> Local employees, unlike Japanese employees, do not consider their work to be the centre of their lives. If push comes to shove, they consider work something they have to do to live. This is where the difficulty lies in expecting local employees to contribute as much to their companies as Japan.[13]

Quoting Orwell, Jetro suggests that labour–management relations in Europe are rooted in class confrontation. Accordingly, only some Japanese practices have been transferred to the UK, with most companies trying instead to accommodate local practices, avoiding potential conflicts. It does not always work. Hitachi, in south Wales, was shocked when a scheme to increase youth employment and to accede to the wishes of a number of older employees seeking voluntary redundancy was widely seen as a Japanese attempt to try to bring in retirement at thirty-five. Tatung – Taiwanese, rather than Japanese – the Shropshire-based computer manufacturer, ran into similar difficulties when in a management memorandum it suggested that supervisors should ensure that employees 'refrain from playing and laughing' at work.

What *has* been transplanted is stability – in companies and in their performance generally, but in industrial relations, too. Stability in Japanese manufacturing is central to improving performance and output, and it is here that the real link between Japanese industrial relations practices and the strike-free deals lies: what they hold out is the prospect of stable, consensual industrial relations, and so of stable company performance, allowing companies to concentrate on production, not on *ad hoc* solutions to keep it going. That was part of the EETPU's pitch when it sent a team of its senior officials to Japan to sell the union to Japanese companies thinking of setting up in the UK; it was a crucial argument when Roy Sanderson and Geoffrey Deith, from Toshiba, were finalising the first of the strike-free agreements – Deith had to sell, and sell hard, to his Japanese masters in the UK and back in Japan, the value of the radical industrial relations package he and Sanderson were trying to establish.

The idea of a whole industrial relations system appealed to the Japanese. Though the interdependence of the elements of the strike-free package seemed to be threatened by the EETPU itself at the end of 1985 in its aborted talks with Rupert Murdoch over Wapping, the reciprocal coherence of the parts of the package is important. To divide them up is to render injustice to the whole, but there are six principal features of the deals. Not every agreement features all of them, and some agreements do so in only very specialised ways, but they provide the core of what is on offer.

Single Unionism

Roy Grantham, the balding, bespectacled general secretary of the white-collar union Apex, is deceptively mild-mannered – he is a tough right-winger, whose union was instrumental in organising the defeat of left-wing unions in elections for TUC General Council seats allocated to organisations with fewer than 100,000 members. But he is thoughtful, too. Others blazed away at the EETPU package; Grantham could see its 'subtle proposals'.[14] Not that such perceptions made him dislike it less: those who signed single-union agreements, he told the 1985 Congress, did so 'to the detriment of their fellow trade unions'.[15] Grantham had not always been so definite. 'The next ten years will see fewer unions as a result of mergers,' he told a managers' conference in 1984. 'It will see fewer bargaining units at companies, and frequently only one at a plant.' He went on to instance such a deal his own union had just signed. At that stage, Grantham proposed to the TUC a regulatory system for single-union deals, based on 'the insurance, "knock-for-knock" principle. If a union benefits as a result of recognised bargaining at one company then when a choice has to be made elsewhere those who earlier lost should benefit.' Within a year, following his own union's ejection from the Hitachi television company in South Wales, Grantham was taking a harder line, calling for the TUC's governing principles on single union deals to be toughened up: 'I believe that today the TUC has to exercise a central responsibility to the movement to reduce excessive and damaging competition between unions – and to prevent rash decisions by employers.'

Grantham was backed up by Tony Dubbins, from the NGA print union – who had also found himself (hardly to his surprise) out in the cold when the EETPU agreed a single-union deal with Eddie Shah for his new national newspaper, *Today*. Sensing a 'widespread concern' about the development of single-union deals, he said they had a 'divisive and disastrous effect on workers' conditions'.[16] Not that the EETPU is the sole beneficiary of such arrangements: despite its promulgation of its own single-union agreements as a model for others to follow, it howled in anguish when the TGWU reached such a deal with the Norsk Hydro energy group, which saw the electricians excluded.

Far from the sole beneficiary, in fact. Although, officially, the TUC and most of its largest affiliate unions are opposed to single-union arrangements, in practice most of its unions – including those most vocally opposed to the idea – have such deals, and are keen to sign more. Estimates vary slightly, but a clear consensus is that a little over 50 per cent of unionised British industry recognises only one union, for its manual workers, though as yet there is no hard evidence on the extent of pure single unionism, where one union reaches an agreement – normally at plant level – to represent all employees, whether manual or non-manual.[17]

Multi-unionism is the norm in British industrial relations. It has its force; it has its proponents. They argue that loyalty to a union, especially where it is craft-based, can create authority, from that discipline, from that efficiency. Perhaps so; but employers who negotiate with a number of unions wearily tell of the sheer time it takes, time which could be well spent more productively than explaining everything several times. Or conversely, multi-unionism is in practice effectively single unionism – a federation, such as the Confederation of Shipbuilding and Engineering Unions, acting as a union, carrying out the negotiations.

Certainly, the EETPU has trumpeted its single-union deals, mainly to bring itself to the notice of employers, so that it can sign more. Other unions, less confident of carrying off such a high-profile strategy, have been more discreet, though they admit privately that they have such agreements, and are reaching more. One clerical union general secretary described how his executive spent some time decrying the moral ignominy of the EETPU for signing single-union deals, until the question was put to it whether or not the union would countenance itself reaching an agreement for sole representation of employees in the area in which it was dominant; silence fell.

One public example involving a union other than the EETPU, which has pressed the case for such deals hardest, is that of Electro Acoustic Industries (Elac), a loudspeaker manufacturer which in 1984 considered moving its operations wholly to South Wales. In London, it eschewed unions, rejecting abruptly an approach from GMBATU in 1981. In thinking about the move to South Wales, the company took advice from Acas and then decided to forestall any recognition campaigns by seeking a deal with GMBATU – the very union it had rebuffed three years earlier. Supported by Acas, Charles Docherty, GMBATU South Wales regional organiser, says: 'I was pleased to go for a one-union agreement because it would mean more membership for us.'[18]

That, precisely, is unions' private practice – in sharp contrast to the public silence which seemed to be the determinant behind the TUC's vote in September 1985 to change its stance. The TUC's formal machinery governing relations between unions, commonly called the Bridlington principles because they were first codified at an annual TUC Congress there in 1939, are the unions' principal method of self-policing. Bridlington now has some legal standing,[19] though it is not fully defined across the whole range of the code's scope; but its principal force is primarily moral – and practical. Breaches are examined by the TUC's disputes committee, whose recommendations are binding. Refusal to acknowledge the committee's decisions can subject unions to disciplinary action – including suspension or even full expulsion from the TUC. Such was the reason for the one-hour suspension of the TGWU over a recognition dispute concerning a Birmingham public house, the Fox and Goose, over which the National Association of Licensed House Managers, tiny by comparison, had just claim.

Significantly, until 1979 the TUC had no rule governing single-union arrangements; it was originally introduced after complaints by public service unions against Nupe (ironically enough, now one of the main critics of the EETPU's deals) over its aggressive recruiting in the 1978–9 winter of discontent disputes. Before then, with union membership expanding, anything other than blatant infringements of the TUC code could be largely forgotten; unions were confident that something like Grantham's knock-for-knock arrangements would unofficially apply. But as the recession bit harder, competition for members grew more intense, and unions began to line themselves up before employers, suitors waiting to be chosen. 'On what basis will an employer decide which union they want?' asked Harry Conroy, of the NUJ. 'Will it be the quietest, or the cheapest?'[20] In an effort to stem fierce infighting for available members, the Wales TUC, with the influx of Japanese and other companies into the Principality, and its northern counterpart, faced with the arrival of Nissan, brought in a degree of further, though still unofficial regulation: all unions could compete for recognition, but once one of them was chosen, all competition should stop. Morgan and Sayer, in a study of new labour relations in South Wales, suggest that this is insufficient, and argue that single unionism is 'profoundly irrational' for unions, adding: 'once one union starts to be successful in such a strategy, others are driven to do the same to counter it.'[21]

Hitachi changed all that. Previously, Principle 1(e), governing single-union deals, simply said that unions should 'have regard to the interests of other unions which may be affected' in making such agreements. But in December 1985, the TUC's employment policy committee approved an amendment to this part of the code, ruling out such deals 'under any circumstances' except by prior consultation and agreement with the other unions concerned. In practice, very few unions would be willing to sign away their negotiating rights to another, unless some very tight unofficial reciprocal agreement has been reached; the effect of the TUC's decision may be to stop such deals dead, or force from its ranks those unions which sign them, or even, as a confidential TUC paper put it, 'lead to a defiance of an ultimatum by an employer that a single-union agreement is necessary to avoid a possible closure of a plant'.[22]

All the EETPU's and other unions' new agreements are single-union. Whatever the TUC says, fewer and fewer employers (especially those foreign-owned, and more especially Japanese) are willing now to sign deals with more than one union – where they are willing to sign them with a union at all. 'The single union agreement must surely become the logical norm,' says Dr MacFarlane of the EEF, 'and not just where they are set up by foreign owners or away from traditional industrial centres.'[23] How far unions are prepared to stick by the TUC's decisions is unclear: 'This is rubbish,' says Bert Lyons, general secretary of the white-collar rail union TSSA, who has not so far signed such a deal. 'If I am in the position where I have 90 per cent membership but there is another union involved, and the employer wants to sign up with us alone, am I going to throw those members away?'

Flexibility

Companies in the recession not only had to cut down on the numbers they employed in order to survive (if they did survive). They had to use their labour more efficiently, and more effectively. Demarcation, a particular bane of British industry, buttressed by the illogically high number of unions, each defending their own craft or other sectional interests, was on the wane: the old definitions of work, the old job titles – a fitter, a spark, a chippie – began to disappear. In their place came jacks of all – or at least of more – trades, craftsmen able to turn their hands to anything their skills could handle.[24] That development marched with increasing technological change and widespread use of computer-based technologies[25] – craftsmen became technicians. For employees and their unions, these developments were a challenge – but an opportunity too, as the engineering union realised:

> For anyone asking themselves where the new work will be in manufacturing industry during the next decade, the answer is plain enough. It will be among the branches of engineering which are already based in electronics and information technology, or which are capable of moving in that direction. So for people who have grown up with traditional mechanical work – and that includes the 2½m-strong population of British engineering – the great issue is whether the changeover is possible or impossible, easy or difficult.[26]

The two strands – harder times and technical change – came together in the key labour market concept of the 1980s: flexibility. With full theoretical support, chiefly from the Institute of Manpower Studies at Sussex University, its principles were reflected in practice. Though fashion is not unimportant in industrial relations – 'no self-respecting personnel manager [would] want to turn up to a management conference or seminar without his or her own flexibility deal firmly under their belt,' said the TUC dismissively[27] – company after company, across a whole range of industries, began to introduce a series of labour practices, revolutionary in themselves, unthinkable five years previously.

Flexibility, in the model defined most notably by John Atkinson at the IMS,[28] takes two principal forms – *numerical* flexibility, in which a company radically alters the traditional composition of a workforce by employing full-time a core group of mainly skilled workers, central to the company's activities, and peripheral groups of less important, often less skilled workers, employed in various and often innovative ways; and *functional* flexibility, in which employees are moved from job to job, depending on their skill match and level. In the strike-free agreements, there are instances of both: Atkinson's most prominent example of flexibility, for instance, is the company formerly known as Control Data, an American-owned computer peripherals firm in South Wales, since taken over by Xidex, which features an unusual strike-free deal with the EETPU.

Functional flexibility is even more common to these agreements – at least partly because the Japanese, and other inward investors, have a particular horror of traditional British demarcations. Further, many of the agreements are in industries where the market demands change, and often quickly. In consumer electronics, for instance, the boom in video recorders in Britain – the UK now features a higher concentration of videos per head of population than even such television-dominated countries as Japan and the USA[29] – meant that UK-based TV manufacturers had rapidly to switch their production lines to meet the changed demand. Such shifts demand a skilled but flexible workforce.

Flexibility is widespread. According to an IMS survey, commissioned by the Department of Employment and the NEDC, almost 90 per cent of manufacturing companies surveyed had sought to increase the functional flexibility of their workforces since 1980.[30] Mostly this was done with workforce approval and support: a MORI poll taken in October 1985 found that 62 per cent of those surveyed felt that willingness to change their job was important, and 64 per cent willingness to undergo retraining; 59 per cent and 64 per cent respectively said that they personally would be ready to carry out such changes, with no lessening of support when broken down to survey trade union members.

Virtually all the strike-free deals feature, almost as an acknowledgement, rather than as a demand, the requirement to be flexible. Take Sanyo:

> All employees are expected to work in any job which they are capable of doing. In-plant training is provided, and job rotation is practised throughout the company. There are no job descriptions, and all production, inspection and most clerical staff are paid the same job salary.

Or Inmos, where unions and management agree to:

> Respond flexibly and quickly to changes in the pattern of demand for the company's products and to technological innovation.

Or Toshiba:

> In reaching this agreement the trade union recognises and supports the complete flexibility of jobs and duties within the company, both within departments and between the various departments of the company, subject to individual skills and capabilities. In return the company recognises and accepts the need for training and retraining in the broadening of skills and in new technological developments as they affect the company's efficiency as a manufacturing operation.'

Or AB Electronics, where both sides agree:

> The maximum co-operation and support from all employees in achieving a completely flexible, well-motivated workforce, capable of transferring on a temporary or permanent basis on to work of any nature, that is within the capabilities of such employees, having due regard to the provisions of adequate training and safety arrangements.

Does it work out that way in practice? Jim Robertson, assistant executive manager for manufacturing engineering at Hitachi, thinks so:

> I used some of our maintenance team to paint the floor of the factory. The important thing about it was that no one thought about it. It wasn't done by forcing people, and it wasn't done at a high level. The guy who asked the guy to paint didn't make a big thing about it. He just said, we've got these lines to get in, and we need some painting done. We'd like you to come in and help us paint. It was no big deal.

Robertson is almost offhand: 'Everybody paints at home. So everybody here just mucks in and does things that they would do in their garage.' But such requests, in other times, in other factories, have led to stoppages, walk-outs, lengthy strikes: no longer. Another manager said: 'We wouldn't ask mechanical people to go and troubleshoot the electrics. But we would certainly ask an electrical man to maybe put up an air pipe – because it happens to be the most convenient job to do at the time.'

Stephen Connock, industrial relations manager with Philips Electronics, suggests that there are three forms of such craft flexibility: core skills, where the basic skill is retained, but the employee has an appreciation of skills required in other jobs; dual skills, where proficiency in another discipline is added to the core skill; and multi-skilling, where a single employee uses a wide-ranging variety of skills.[31] There are clear benefits to the employee in such developments: Roy Sanderson of the EETPU emphasises that retraining acquired at a company covered by one of the electricians' deals (although it is not as extensive in practice as he hoped it would be) improves the employee's *external* job marketability, while the TUC acknowledges that flexibility deals do contain some attractive features – job enhancement, improved work organisation, greater personal involvement. The attractiveness for employers is clear, too: the Technical Change Centre estimates that 'a traditional manual plant with the typical departmental empires with managerial and other demarcations can with the full adoption of an integrated and flexible organisation reduce manning levels by 20–30 per cent,' improving machine efficiencies by 10–15 per cent and increasing machine speeds by 20–65 per cent.[32]

It is this aspect which most worries the unions – or at least some of them. The TUC sees flexibility as 'a cloak behind which to get up to some very old-fashioned tricks', and a term covering a range of 'unattractive and dangerous developments'. It sees functional flexibility, for instance, primarily as a device which leads 'more or less to straightforward intensifications of work and loss of skill. The failure of training systems to keep pace with changing work patterns and technologies leads – against a background of inadequate public provision – to a further impoverishment of skill levels. It can also in extreme cases pose health and safety risks.'[33]

The list of flexibility deals – apart from those covered by strike-free agreements – was by the beginning of 1986 extensive: among them Babcock Power, Perkins of Shrewsbury, Anglesey Aluminium, Esso tanker drivers, Caterpillar Tractor, Borg Warner, Shell Carrington and Shell Stanlow, Findus at Long Benton, ICL, Cadbury at Chirk, Eaton's, Nabisco, Scottish & Newcastle, Colman's, Mobil Coryton.

Take Shell's Carrington plant, in Manchester. The deal, signed in July 1985, saved from closure the company's largest chemicals plant – at the cost of the loss of 700 jobs. Under the terms of the agreement, the structure of fourteen craft groups like welders, plumbers and laggers was swept away. Three former grading structures for white-collar staff, craftsmen and the TGWU were forged into one. All non-management personnel, even including clerical and catering staff, were reclassified as technicians on a nine-grade pay system, and three of the seven unions previously on the site saw their bargaining rights rescinded. No longer will an electrician changing a lamp have to wait for a rigger to set up a climbing frame. The company expects to have every plant technician sufficiently skilled to deal with about 80 per cent of traditional craftsmen's work across all traditional trades.[34]

Or take Borg Warner, the automatic transmission company, in South Wales. Its deal, agreed at the same time, was astonishing:

saving about 600 jobs, and keeping open the plant, it provided a pay agreement covering the following six years to 1991, one of the longest of the growing UK trend of pay deals running for more than the traditional twelve months. Flexibility provisions included an extension of operators' responsibilities to cover inspection, minor maintenance, tool set-ups and changes, machine lubrication, and machine and work-area cleaning. 'We're trying to get away from the concept of competition between management and employees,' said Paul Humphries, the company's divisional personnel manager, 'and replace it with competition between ourselves, and our competitors.'[35]

Single Status

Trudging into work from the third car park (manual), past the second (office) and first (management), or eating in the canteen, rather than the restaurant, or the dining room, the small, cumulative and often frictional differences in the quality of working life are apparent. 'The so-called manual worker', the chairman of the Electricity Council said in 1967, 'was treated as slightly different from and slightly inferior to his colleagues, clerical, administrative and technical. We regarded this as an anachronism. Many so-called manual jobs carry as great a responsibility as an office job.'[36] The Electricity Council was one of the most prominent organisations to conclude a status agreement in the more open, egalitarian days of the 1960s. For many companies, such ambitions – if they were ever that, and not just responses to pressures from trade unions able to exert them – have long faded. Maurice Phelps is the board member for personnel industrial relations in British Shipbuilders, and while he was with Shell in the 1960s was part of that company's drive for bridging the status divisions: 'We spent a considerable amount of time developing harmonisation and single status. Many companies are in fact no further forward now than we were then.' On BS's own programme, he says: 'We have a harmonisation programme in the shipbuilding industry, and I think the unions would agree we have had to put it on a back burner in the last four or five years.' Paul Dixon, director of personnel with the North Thames division of British Gas, says his impression is that a 'significant proportion' of companies 'regarded the matter as of low priority'.[37]

Harmonisation and single status are not the same. Harmonisation is generally gradualistic, narrowing the difference in the basis of treatment of broad groups of employees; single status is an absolute equivalence of terms and conditions for all employees, often – though certainly not always – introduced on greenfield sites, by foreign-owned companies, and likely to be found in capital-intensive, highly technological industrial sectors.[38] Indeed, many companies, and especially those which are Japanese-owned, do not use the term 'single status'; the Japanese in particular are highly status-conscious, and clearly regard *single* status as unthinkable. Status is an attitude of mind, an abstract concept – not something connected with how companies treat their employees. Such companies prefer to describe their initiatives as 'common terms and conditions'. For the Japanese, that extends to all parts of the company, most obviously to the uniforms – usually short tunics – which all employees wear. But that practice, though generally insisted upon, is generally consensual.[39] At Hitachi, for instance, as part of the negotiations for its agreement with the EETPU, the company had a number of designs made up of proposed company jackets, and the workforce was able to reach a decision on the design it preferred.

Most of the companies which have reached strike-free agreements feature common terms and conditions. Take Optical Fibres, the Deeside-based joint venture between BICC, the UK's leading cable manufacturer, and the Canadian company Corning Glass. The company reached in January 1983 a deal with EESA, the autonomous staff section of the EETPU. In the factory, first names are used by all employees – including management. There are no differences between clerical and manufacturing workers on holiday entitlements, sickness benefit, pensions, and the provision of private medical insurance. Cloakrooms and the restaurant are used by all. The car park has no reserved spaces. Every employee – including the plant's general manager – signs on daily in a reception register on arrival and departure; there is no clocking on or off.

These practices are the norm in a number of other establishments, too – such as Continental Can, in Wrexham (whose personnel and industrial relations director, Peter Wickens, took many of his ideas with him when he went further north to another foreign-owned company, this time Japanese – Nissan), or Johnson & Johnson, the pharmaceuticals company, or Sheffield City Council, or CMG, the Croydon-based computer group.[40] Many have moved towards single status for pure commercial reasons, for the cause of greater efficiency: as the need for labour flexibility grows, and as the job content distinctions between the old blue- and white-collar groupings become increasingly blurred, the *employer's* requirement for closer or common terms and conditions comes into line with the long-held but little-realised aspirations of employees and their unions.

For the employer, single status clearly helps to secure co-operative attitudes and some degree of common purpose and commitment from the workforce, improvements in morale – as well as in pay (through grading) and general remuneration on holidays and sickness and other benefits. But it is not smooth, or simple, and not perfect either. Sometimes, it draws rooted opposition from traditional white-collar workers and their unions, and sometimes it simply works differently in practice. At Hitachi, for instance, on a site visit in October 1985, the visitors' car park, right next to the factory, seemed surprisingly full for a plant which had no other visitors that day. Alun Jones, industrial relations manager of Sony's well-established – ten years – plant at nearby Bridgend in South Wales spoke to a closed Acas management–union seminar that month in Cardiff on his company's own experience, questioning whether, for instance, it was fair and reasonable for there to be equal treatment of employees when there was not equal responsibility. He also noted that in Sony's single-status restaurant, the walls were no longer there, but some of the barriers still were – managers ate with managers, lineworkers with lineworkers, rugby players with rugby players, Japanese with Japanese. The title of his address? 'Single status – in pursuit of the Holy Grail!' Maybe so; but the strike-free agreements, and others, *are* in pursuit; many UK companies have still to get away from the starting line.

Participation

Since 1979, industrial democracy has become a devalued, or at least a changed, concept. In the 1970s, under a Labour Government, and fired by the visionary belief of Jack Jones, then general secretary of the TGWU, industrial democracy grew from an idea, long-held but never achieved, first into an inquiry, from that into the Bullock Report, from that into a White Paper, from that to two notable areas of practice – the Post Office and British Steel – and from that: nothing.[41] With the Conservative Government's accession to office in 1979, which coincided with Jones' retirement, the momentum for industrial democracy, certainly in the mechanistic, Bullock sense of workers sitting on company boards, slowed at first to an embarrassed shuffle (in the two nationalised industries) and pretty soon, there as elsewhere, to a halt. Management's right to manage became the new watchword, better suited, companies thought, to leaner times. Vestiges dribbled on: the requirement in the Government's 1982 Employment Act upon companies with more than 250 employees to provide in their annual reports a statement on action taken to introduce, maintain or develop employee participation; the Vredeling and fifth directives from the EEC for greater employee participation, though both were bitterly opposed by the Government. The Conservatives' preferred form of employee participation was *financial* – workers buying shares in their employing companies, linking power and responsibility, commitment and risk. The advantageous terms offered to the employees of British Telecom when its shares were offered for sale in 1984 were only the most prominent example. But poll evidence indicates that share ownership among employees is low – MORI puts it at 9 per cent overall, and lower among trade unionists (5 per cent).

Some employers, rubbing across the grain, persisted. Roland Long, of International Harvester, told a conference in 1984:

> Successful employee involvement will lead to a condition of total commitment to the success of the enterprise. For the first time, management and managed will be part of the same team, working to the same ends. In this kind of situation the scope for industrial disputes will certainly be drastically reduced, if not completely eliminated.[42]

Communication became much more the vogue, in a plethora of forms: quality circles, team briefings, cascade briefings, training programmes, informal drinks with the managers, newssheets, company videos, home postal shots, individual ballots, opinion surveys. Nevertheless, all this communication did not seem to have been wholly successful. According to MORI, 64 per cent of trade union members believe that the information provided by management is unfairly slanted, to tell employees only what the company wishes them to know. Further, 53 per cent of union members believe that management only *started* to tell them about the company's economic position when news of it was bad.

In that sense, what the strike-free agreements offer – real involvement, real information, real participation – runs against the tide. Central to them all is a form of joint council which reaches decisions on a wide range of employee-related issues, on the basis of the provision of the fullest possible information, which if accepted by the company (and the strong moral force of decisions reached in this way certainly predisposes the company to accept them) becomes company policy. Called different names under different agreements – a company members' board at Hitachi, an advisory council at Inmos; a company advisory board at Sanyo and at Toshiba; a joint negotiating council at AB Electronics, a company council at Nissan – all work to the same principles and share the same aims; all stem from the same root.

Geoffrey Deith was the managing director of Rank-Toshiba when the joint Anglo-Japanese venture went out of business in 1980. Previously, and now again, with Rank alone, Deith had envisioned the idea of an advisory board for some time. The collapse of the company, though catastrophic, gave him the opportunity to put it into practice in the new company which was to rise, Phoenix-like, from the joint venture's ashes. Roy Sanderson from the EETPU, the officer given the task to negotiate redundancy terms for those being shed, had *his* notions too. From their combination was born the Toshiba agreement which, in turn, spawned the other strike-free deals. 'When I was negotiating the Toshiba agreement,' Sanderson says now, 'it was the management who proposed the advisory board – and I was against it. I was against it because it would have allowed non-union people to sit on the board. I wanted the workers' representation confined to trade unionists, but the company did not agree, and eventually I acceded.'

Deith and Sanderson applied their own separate strands of thinking about the redundancy of institutionalised conflict in industry to the questions of industrial democracy, participation and involvement. 'There are enormous areas of business in which there are common interests between shareholder and employee,' wrote Deith in an unpublished background Toshiba paper on the advisory board system, 'and the remaining areas are capable of satisfactory solution providing both parties are able and willing to seek solutions which are of mutual benefit. The Company Advisory Board system provides the forum in which such solutions can be found.'[43]

Sceptics of the system suggest that there is nothing new in it, that it is simply an updated form of the old works council, a talking shop, no teeth, impotent. Deith's view was far from that:

> It should not be seen as primarily a means of problem solving in a company, although this may often happen. Rather, through a process of the expression of views, knowledge of relevant information and the application of common sense, difficulties can be anticipated and solutions found before a problem has arisen. In this way the traditional practice of waiting for a problem to arise, and resolving it through conflict, becomes either unnecessary or a process of last resort.

He stresses the nature of the board: 'The board's function is advisory, and therefore does not seek to compromise the shareholders' position, but experience shows that providing the board is equipped with adequate information, and experienced in its function, then the advice is more effective than the few votes of worker directors or the threats of organised sectors of the company's employees.'

To that end, the advisory board is broadly based, drawing its members from occupational groups. Though it has changed as the company has grown, the Toshiba advisory board has the following configuration (before the inclusion of representatives from its separate, but linked, microwave-oven plant):

Chairman:	Managing director
Company representative:	Manufacturing director
Secretary:	Personnel director

Members (with voting rights):

1. VCR final assembly and test
2. Machine shop, stores
3. Chassis
4. Flat pack
5. Final test and packing
6. Panel assembly 1
7. Panel assembly 2
8. Maintenance and technical
9. Administration
10. Main line
11. Sub-assembly
12. Supervision
13. Supervision/administration
14. Management
15. Senior shop steward (if not already an elected member)

Plus – Observers from the factory (non-voting)
– Senior managers not otherwise present (non-voting)

When it meets, there are no pre-meetings, among management or workforce representatives, no predetermined position. Employee representatives – not necessarily trade union representatives – give the board prior advice arising out of their knowledge and experience in the factory and outside it.

Clearly, the unions have only a tangential impact on a structure such as this; there is a tension between the advisory board system and the trade union structure. But that may not be unpopular: MORI suggests, for instance, that only 28 per cent of trade union members believe that management should only communicate with the shop-floor through official union channels. Deith is specific:

> The role of the trade union in representing individual members in cases of grievance, discipline or other individual matters affecting their employment is not affected. The trade union recognises that CoAB [Company Advisory Board] debate must be the first stage within the company on any matter related to terms and conditions of employment. The traditional role of the trade union in collective bargaining can then be taken up if any issue is not resolved as a result of CoAB discussion.

For the advisory board to work, the company has to be open and honest with it – it must willingly release confidential financial information to the board to allow it to make its decisions. Sometimes, decisions will not easily be reached – but Deith envisaged that decisions *would* always be reached:

> The basic assumption of the system is that, given adequate information and the right attitude of both company and employees, then in all situations there is a right course of action which is of mutual benefit to company and employees. It may take time and several meetings on a given topic for the company to move its position or for the advisory board to reconsider its position, but eventually the advice of the CoAB will be acceptable to the company and implementation will follow.

If not, then the whole system moves on – towards arbitration. But at all times, the emphasis is on reporting back – to employees, to managers too, by promptly agreed, jointly produced minutes, widely distributed, and by individual briefings from board members.

What does such a board consider? In yielding the principle of non-union CoAB members, Roy Sanderson of the EETPU secured something else: 'One of the points I made in conceding that was that there should be no holds barred, any subject could be discussed. If they wanted to discuss the managing director's car, they could.' Toshiba agreed with the EETPU a list of subjects which would first be raised at the advisory board:

- Company investment policy and business plans
- Company trading performance
- Company operating efficiency
- Company manpower plans and stability of employment
- Terms and conditions of employment, including pay and benefits, and conditions of service
- Work environment and conditions

What do employees in the company then get told of the board's decisions? Hitachi runs for its employees, or company members, a similar system to Toshiba. After one routine meeting of its board in 1985 – not a major meeting about pay, this is what was issued to employees:

> *Minutes of Company Members' Board Meeting Held Monday 28 October at 10.30 a.m.*
>
> Training
>
> Concern was expressed at the lack of training for new Company Members, and it was felt that this was contributing to the number of rejects currently being experienced in production. It was also felt that due to lack of a training facility, more experienced Members were being moved, while new Members were allowed to stay in the same job to gain experience. The CMB also expressed concern at the lack of training for all members. While they agreed with the principle of flexibility, they felt that without training, flexibility will fail. They recommended that Members be trained to perform various tasks so that they could then be transferred with confidence, and enable the principle of flexibility to work. The company realises the need for more training and to provide people to carry out training.

Discipline

Again the CMB were concerned with the way in which the disciplinary procedure was being administered – mainly that the administration was not uniform from department to department. The CMB also felt that an element of pettiness was now creeping into the administration of such procedure, with a failure to treat Members as adults. It was felt that these problems were leading to the feeling of low morale now present in the company.

The company has also realised there are problems in this area and has instigated monthly meetings for team leaders and middle management. These meetings commenced on the 28 and 29 October, respectively. The first area to be covered was Absence and Overtime Management. It is hoped that by taking these steps many of the problems voiced at the CMB will be overcome.

Production Efficiency

While the CMB agrees that Members need to increase their efficiency, they also felt that other factors affected efficiency, and were not considered sufficiently when measuring efficiency.

Other factors were:

(a) Material shortages
Material shortages such as the one currently experienced on tubes, were felt to play a large part in falls in efficiency.

Steps are being taken by the purchasing department to avoid material shortages in the future. They are now pursuing a policy of 'dual sourcing'. Under such a system, there will always be at least two sources for all such materials required.

(b) Design
It was felt that new models were put into pre-production on the lines before they were ready. This has led to modifications being carried out at the same time as production. This does not help efficiency.

A number of steps have been taken by the company to improve this situation. In future, pre-production models will not be mixed in with production models. Also recruitment is now being carried out to strengthen the design department.

Company members' handbook

This is now at the printers and should be available for issue during November.

The company also plans to hold a series of information meetings in the new year for all company members.

CMB's effectiveness

A complaint was made against the effectiveness of the CMB. Mainly that although problems are pointed out to the CMB, they are very slow to solve them. It was felt that the CMB had become bogged down with administration.

The other main complaint was that when problems were pointed out to the CMB as a result of the shop stewards and representatives meetings, the company frequently replied that it knew of the problem and was taking steps to deal with it. It was felt that the company should have brought these problems to the CMB rather than waiting for them to come from the shop stewards/representatives meeting.

This complaint was answered by the management, pointing out that significant improvements have been made in the terms and conditions of employees, in the short space of time since the commencement of Hitachi Consumer Products UK Ltd. It was felt that the current terms and conditions were second to none, but this was not to say that there was no room for improvement.

Next meeting

The next meeting will be held during week commencing 11.11.85.

At this meeting the following will be discussed:

(1) Reply from company on grading structure.
(2) Report on meeting with WDA re car parking facilities.

Meeting 18 Commenced: 10.30 a.m. Finished: 12.00 p.m.

31 October 1985

What this clearly shows is a workforce, and a company, raising problems and reaching agreement on how best to respond to them – co-operatively. The difference between the advisory board and, say, normal company consultation procedures is in the role of the board: its advice forms the basis of company decisions; workforce representatives have a genuine say in how the company operates, not just at the level of their own effort, but beyond it, on policy. It also shows imperfections and disgruntlements with the system (though it may be a positive feature of it that it can handle such wrinkles). But giving detailed information to representatives of the employees, and bringing them into the process of decision-making, runs against the trend on information (40 per cent of trade union members have no idea how much, if any, profit their employing company makes). And by making clear the real commonality of interest between employer and employee – the survival of the company – the relationship between risk and commitment is properly comprehended, and the company becomes more fully integrated, more efficient and more effective.

Pendulum Arbitration

Pendulum arbitration is at the heart of the strike-free agreements – and is their most controversial feature. Its use as a strike substitute by the EETPU, and by the other unions involved is at the centre of the charges of ceding the right to strike brought against the EETPU in particular by many of its union opponents. Yet if that is its function, it is surprising that it should draw opposition, since strikes are generally seen as negative: MORI found in October 1985 that 41 per cent of those surveyed saw strikes as mainly to blame for British industry's low growth rate, just behind overseas competition. Significantly, the figures for trade union members showed little difference. Further, 51 per cent (49 per cent of trade union members) thought that the avoidance of strikes was important to shopfloor workers' employment security.

What, then, is pendulum arbitration – or straight-choice, or final-offer, or even 'flip-flop' arbitration, as it is also known? Toshiba's agreement, the first of the strike-free deals to feature it, puts it clearly:

> The terms of reference of the arbitrator will be to find in favour of either the company or the trade union. A compromise solution shall not be recommended.

Under conventional arbitration, a dispute which is not being resolved by industrial action but which has failed to be solved by negotiation (where the two sides talk together), or by conciliation (where a third party helps the two sides to reach agreement), or by mediation (where a third party makes recommendations as a basis for negotiations by the two sides), is resolved by a third party drawing up a settlement. Strictly, all arbitration should by definition be binding, though the idea of 'binding' arbitration, as opposed to a less deterministic 'non-binding' form, is now growing in industrial relations practice.

Conventional arbitration tends, then, to be a compromise, in which, as Sir John Wood, chairman of the Government's Central Arbitration Committee, puts it, the best arbitrations tend to disappoint both parties slightly. The CAC acknowledges that 'critics of this approach have complained that in practice arbitrators are tempted merely to split the difference'[44] between the two sides, though Sir John, also professor of law at Sheffield University, dismisses this as a 'misconception'.[45] Acas, the leading UK industrial relations arbitration body, does not publish the results of its arbitrations in terms of which side, in the main, its awards tended to favour – management or employees. But an internal, unpublished 1981 Acas survey found that only 7 per cent of awards 'split the difference' – that is, fell within the mid-50 per cent band between the employer's last-known offer and the union's last-known claim.[46] Indeed, according to an internal note by the Department of Employment, the 'experience is that awards frequently come down in the employers' favour'.[47] Right enough; a further internal Acas estimate is that about 10 per cent of arbitrations settle at the company's final offer.

But such findings have not deflected the Conservative Government from a drive against arbitration, and in particular against arbitration featuring unilateral access – the right of either side to elect to go to arbitration. In 1981, the Cabinet's secret economic committee reviewed arbitration across the entire public sector, and, according to a Cabinet paper, concluded that 'the only sure way for employers to avoid the risk of awards they cannot afford is to refuse to go to arbitration. It follows that arbitration should not take place without their consent, but only on mutual agreement.' The paper suggested that 'the main defect in many current arrangements is that they provide unilateral access to arbitration; and . . . this right should be re-negotiated, or if necessary withdrawn'.[48] Since then, the Government has in practice done precisely that, holding out against arbitration in the lengthy mid-1980s teachers' dispute, or refusing it altogether in the Civil Service. For civil servants, it was suggested in late 1985 that the only form of arbitration ministers had any interest at all in countenancing was pendulum arbitration.

They were not alone. After News International's flit to Wapping, other newspaper managements started proposing new agreements built around pendulum arbitration. Further, following the signing of a number of strike-free deals, the right-wing Institute of Directors embraced the concept of pendulum arbitration as a means (explained Sir John Hoskyns, IoD director-general) both of reaching a new consensus in industry by the use of 'agreed and reasonable' procedures, and of rebuffing the 'resurgence of the "British disease"' which the IoD detected in the miners' and associated strikes. The IoD praised the EETPU as 'leaders in the field' – much to the disgust of the EETPU. Roy Sanderson said: 'I am convinced the IoD does not have the same intention that we have. They appear to be looking for some restrictive agreement on industrial relations whereas our agreements are designed to enhance the collective and individual rights of workers.' Yet the IoD maintained that 'recent moves by some companies and unions towards "no-strike" agreements suggest that the climate of labour relations in Britain may be starting to change.' Of pendulum arbitration itself, the IoD said: 'There have been suggestions that such a system would not be suited to the industrial relations climate in Britain; that we are too used to conventional arbitration for the results of final-offer arbitration to be satisfactory. The Institute does not believe that this is necessarily the case.'[49]

With good reason: despite appearances, particularly the erroneous belief that pendulum arbitration is a Japanese practice, straight-choice arbitration is not new in the UK. 'There are many arbitrations which require arbitrators to make a straight choice, and they have done for years,' says Dennis Boyd, Acas' chief conciliation officer. Figure 6.1, drawn from an internal Acas survey, proves his point.[50] Figures for 1984 (24 per cent straight choice) and for the first nine months of 1985 (29 per cent) are broadly similar. Many straight-choice arbitrations cannot be anything else: in a grading dispute, for instance, an employee is either going to be made up a grade or he is not; no compromise choice is possible.

Pendulum arbitration in the strike-free deals, though, did not flower from these examples, but from Roy Sanderson's discovery of the practice in America. 'Conventional arbitration had become discredited,' Sanderson says. 'We've had a number of instances – say, railways or wherever – where an arbitrator has produced an award that's then been condemned by both parties, utterly condemned; and far from improving industrial relations, very often the arbitrator's award has done the opposite.' Sanderson came across the theory, and practice, of pendulum arbitration in the USA, but in fact its roots are probably British – in the wages councils, the system of collective

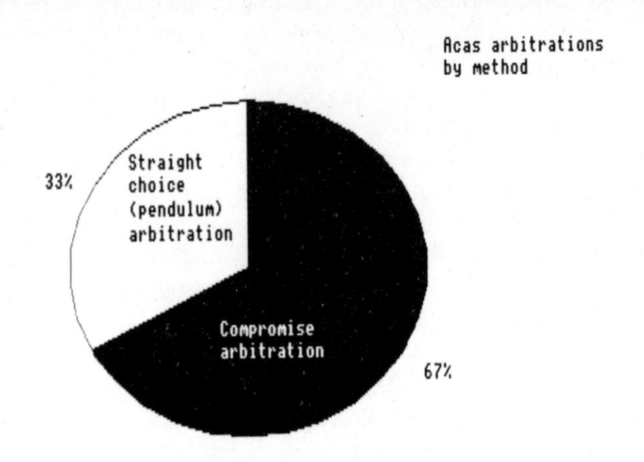

Figure 6.1: Pendulum arbitration - UK practice Source: Acas

bargaining which applies to about 2.7 million UK workers, many of them low-paid, in areas such as retailing or clothing manufacture. A wages council has three sides – employers, employees and independent members. If agreement is not reached between the employer and employees, each in turn appeals to the independent members. The issue is finally resolved by a vote, providing in effect for the independent members to choose wholly one or the other.

The similarities were acknowledged by the man regarded now as the originator of pendulum arbitration, Carl Stevens, professor of economics at Reed College, Oregon. Stevens was steeped in the game theory of bluff and tactics, usually applied to international relations and the study of conflict,[51] and in his 1963 work *Strategy and Collective Bargaining Negotiation* attempted to apply its analysis to wage bargaining and industrial relations. His little-known, though startling work contained within it the seeds of pendulum arbitration – in particular his juxtaposition of the employees' minimum demand and the employers' maximum offer. Three years later, he drew these loose strands together in a trail-blazing article, 'Is Compulsory Arbitration Compatible with Bargaining?'

Stevens examined the strike functionally:

> The strike is a technique by means of which each party may impose a cost of disagreement on the other. The central role usually assigned to the strike in the analysis of collective bargaining is predicated upon the notion that a technique for imposing a cost of disagreement is necessary to invoke the processes of concession and compromise which are an essential part of normal collective bargaining negotiations. In principle, a cost of disagreement might be imposed in other ways.[52]

He suggested that the threat of arbitration might stimulate compromise and concession. In fact what tends to happen is that, if there is a prospect of a move to arbitration, the employer holds back financially at least a little, both believing that a lower final offer will lead an arbitrator to pitch an award lower and knowing he will need to retain money to fund the award when it comes; this has become known, especially in America, as the 'chilling' effect of arbitration on normal negotiations.

Faced with this effect, Stevens came up with what he called the 'one-or-the-other criterion' for replacing the strike as the mechanism for imposing the cost of disagreement:

> Generally speaking, this criterion generates just the kind of uncertainty about the location of the arbitration award that is well calculated to recommend maximum notions of prudence to the parties and, hence, compel them to seek security in agreement. Moreover, under this criterion – and unlike the case under the compromise criterion – there is no reason to suppose that big claims may be rewarded and concessions penalized. Indeed, expectations may tend to be the other way round, as each party may assume that the arbitrator will reject an 'exaggerated' position in favour of an opponent's more moderate claim.[53]

That is exactly what the proponents of pendulum arbitration in the UK's strike-free deals – particularly Sanderson of the EETPU – claim for it: the prospect of a dispute going to pendulum arbitration, of one side wholly winning or wholly losing, feeds back into the negotiations, making them more realistic, forcing each side to draw towards each other – and so towards a settlement – rather than be left in the event of a disagreement with a position more unreasonable

than the other side's, and so more likely not to be the choice of the arbitrator.

So far in the UK, the theory has not been fully tested in hard workplace practice. In the USA, where the system has been in place for some time – twelve states now use it – the position is different. Research covering the first eight years of the system's operation in Iowa shows that most cases are settled by normal negotiation, but of those that are not, as Figure 6.2 shows, only a tiny proportion go on to pendulum arbitration, suggesting that it may well be true that it promotes reasonableness on both sides, and so increases the likelihood of a settlement.[54] A further study, describing an experiment under which industrial relations students were divided up into 'union' and 'management', also showed a clear convergence between the two sides: the gap between opening and final claims and offers for those negotiating normally remained wide, but the difference between 'union' and 'management' when negotiations faced the prospect of pendulum arbitration was tiny.[55]

Pendulum arbitration in the USA is mostly used in the public sector, often covering employees such as fire and police officers who

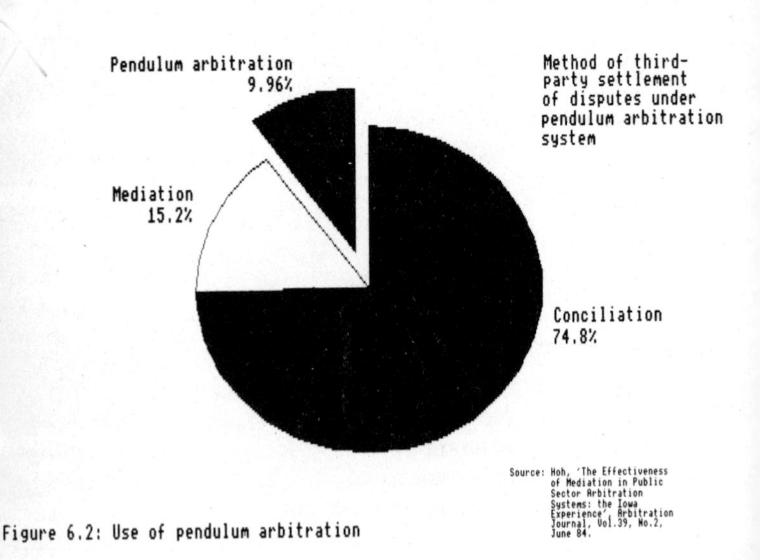

Figure 6.2: Use of pendulum arbitration

are prohibited by law from striking. It has not spread into the private sector (unlike in the UK, where the reverse is the case) apart from one notable example – professional major league baseball. Though it covers only a very small number of employees – each of the eighteen major teams has a roster of about twenty-four players – the application of the system has meant that the money involved is now huge: in 1969 the average salary for a major-league player was about $28,000, but in 1984 it had risen to about $379,000. In an effort to contain spiralling wage costs among players, the employers brought in pendulum arbitration, but after a key test case in which the arbitrator chose the salary claim for one player of $1 million in preference to his team's offer of $700,000, the system has now led to vast salary increases, provoking scepticism about its value among team owners. But such experience has brought in important refinements to the basic system. These have included prefacing it with UK-style mediation; providing a fact-finder's report as a third option for the arbitrator; allowing each side to submit an alternative final offer or claim, to give the arbitrator four options; or issue-by-issue pendulum arbitration, whereby the arbitrator selects specific points from each side's final position.

Such few British examinations of the system as there have been also have their reservations. Acas publicly expressed only 'great interest' in the strike-free deals[56]; privately, its internal report on them says they have 'substantial' potential benefits, especially for employers.[57] Acas suggests that their success depends on a high degree of initial trust between the parties, says that pendulum arbitration 'will not be readily applicable to all industries and all issues', and indicates that awards arising from pendulum arbitration 'may not necessarily stand the test of fairness or improve relations in the longer term'.[58] The Central Arbitration Committee insists that it is essential for arbitrations to maintain a degree of flexibility, to avoid the dilemma in which neither the offer nor the claim which are the subject of the arbitration is without serious flaw.[59] Sir John Wood, the CAC's chairman, makes this point himself and remarks sceptically:

> It is difficult to determine what is the last offer; it is artificial to hold the parties to their last offer, for if final agreement is preferable to an award, so a movement closer together, even at the last minute, has to be welcome. Few cases involve only one simple issue. Once there is complexity or multiplicity then

difficulties arise. The solutions, such as splitting the issues, strike at the fundamental purpose of the reform.[60]

Finally, Professor Sid Kessler, called in to Sanyo to mediate in the first real test of the UK strike-free deals' procedures, suggests that pendulum arbitration does not guarantee that the arbitrator's award 'will necessarily meet tests of fairness and equity', and is particularly pointed about the system's preclusion of one of arbitration's traditional, though little-stated, roles: face-saving. He says: 'Pendulum arbitration prevents this, because one side is openly seen to "win" and the other to "lose". No compromise is possible. For one side to defeat totally the other is not a basis for continuing stable and orderly relations.'

These are valid points, though to some extent they are the complaints of professional arbitrators about a system which is based on perceived defects in conventional arbitration, as practised by them, and which is in fact aimed at reducing recourse to arbitration, not increasing it. At any rate, they are points which the practitioners of the system recognise. Sanderson in particular, having learnt more about the complexities now offered in the American use of the form, believes that there is scope for modifying the agreements; indeed, he and the EETPU stress that it is against the whole nature of the deals for them to be rigid, to remain fixed – they should respond in changing industries to changing circumstances.

He is convinced of the value of pendulum arbitration for three principal reasons. First, because it is less costly, less damaging than the strikes for which it is the substitute. Secondly, because it is 'recession-proof' – in that the decision is not based on purely economic factors, but on the soundness of the argument presented. Finally, because the strike is an unfair mechanism, in that 'it settles the differences not on the basis of natural justice, but on the basis of a trial of strength. You can have the best case in the world, but if you've got no industrial muscle, you'll lose the strike. You can have the worst case in the world but if you've got industrial muscle you can win the strike.' Under pendulum arbitration, the case that seems most just should carry the day, no matter how industrially weak in traditional union muscle terms the employees might be – unusually in terms of traditional industrial relations, muscle does not necessarily mean money; might does not always mean right.

No-Strike Provisions

Strikes can be prevented – by law. Indeed, by law passed by a Labour Government. As part of its 'social contract' with the unions of the mid-1970s – a package of legislative reform in return for agreement to a restrictive incomes policy – Labour brought to the statute book the Trade Union and Labour Relations Act 1974. Section 18(4) of the Act provides for a collective agreement between management and its employees to prohibit or restrict the right of workers to engage in a strike or other industrial action, as long as it is in line with a number of tests: that the agreement is a written one; that it expressly states that such a no-strike provision shall or may be incorporated in the agreement; that the agreement is reasonably accessible at the workplace and available for consultation; and that the union party to it is an independent trade union, as defined by the Act. Like many employment law provisions, this section remains in force – but it has been wholly unused since its enactment (though there had been a similar case of a contractual no-strike deal, with the state airline, then called BOAC), because no union would be likely to agree to it.

But some employees *are* legally prevented from striking: since 1797, the armed forces, under a range of statutes; and since 1919, the police, currently under the 1964 Police Act, plus other statutes for some local forces.[61] Until 1971, it was a criminal offence under the Conspiracy and Protection of Property Act 1875 for gas, water or electricity workers to break their employment contracts (for instance, by going on strike) if the consequence was that customers would be without supply, unless they gave due notice, usually of a week, or their intention to do so. Merchant seamen can only take industrial action if they give twenty-four hours' notice and their vessel is securely moored in a safe berth. The legal position of postal and telecommunications workers is unclear: provisions intended to deter individual acts of industrial misconduct may have the effect of making any industrial action unlawful, though the official view is that they remain free to strike, but not to take discriminatory action against individual customers.

No employees, in fact, have a legal *right* to strike: the laws governing strikes, and other forms of industrial action, are based on a system of legal immunities which protect unions from liability from legal action under circumstances which the Conservative Government has narrowed considerably. That does not at all diminish the widespread belief that there is a right to strike, a fundamental one, and that for workers to yield it voluntarily is not only industrially foolhardy, but ill-judged in terms of the preservation of civil liberties.

Nevertheless, there are a number of examples of the voluntary restriction of strikes. One of the longest-running, and a clear forerunner of the provisions in the new, strike-free agreements, is the scheme covering the electrical contracting industry agreed in 1966 and operational since 1968. The agreement between the contracting employers and the electricians' union set up a Joint Industry Board, with subsidiary regional boards, to regulate industrial relations. The national board has fourteen representatives appointed by the Electrical Contractors' Association, and ten by the EETPU – including Eric Hammond, the general secretary. If a dispute breaks out, it can, if it remains unresolved, be referred to the regional boards for joint settlement; failure to reach agreement at that level moves it to the national board, if necessary for settlement by the vote of the chairman. While the dispute is being examined, the union would not take official industrial action; nor would it sanction unofficial action. Other examples include: the 1972 agreement between the American company, Marathon Manufacturing, and the unions at the Clydebank yard of Upper Clyde Shipbuilders, which included compulsory, binding arbitration; the retail meat industry, where differences still unsettled after negotiation and conciliation are referred to Acas for binding arbitration; and the slag industry, which also has a provision for mandatory arbitration.[62]

Binding arbitration is also a feature of industrial relations abroad – for instance, in Australia, where it has been a hallmark of labour relations since the turn of the century.

Some unions, too, have voluntarily given up the 'right' to strike. The Royal College of Nursing, for instance, declares as a policy that its members will not take strike action, as does the Professional Association of Teachers (both successful, rapidly growing unions; both outside the TUC). The latter's note of guidance to members on industrial action says: 'The cardinal rule of PAT is that no member shall take part in a strike.'

In one of the few union considerations of the strike-free agreements, the TUC in a confidential document suggests that the range of procedure agreements commonplace throughout British industry, which provide for the conduct of negotiations and the handling of grievances and disputes, are roughly equivalent to the new, strike-free deals because they contain no-strike or lock-out provisions.[63] A 1983 internal Acas survey looked at a total of 558 procedure agreements, and broadly confirmed the TUC's thoughts about no-strike and lock-out provisions. Acas found that 84 per cent of those surveyed had disputes procedures, with 85 per cent providing for third-party intervention (87 per cent of these stipulating Acas).[64] The survey found that 72 per cent of the procedure agreements contained *status quo*/no-strike clauses. The fundamental misconception in the TUC's paper, though, was not to realise that the unique characteristic of the strike-free package is that it provides an inexhaustible procedure, which, when linked to the precise strictures against strikes, makes stoppages highly unlikely. Ordinary procedure agreements do not feature this, as Acas found: of those with a *status quo*/no-strike clause, 86 per cent saw it expire after the stage of third-party intervention – effectively sanctioning a strike, or a lock-out, to take place.

There have been two especially prominent proposals for limiting employees' ability to strike – prominent perhaps only because they were rejected. One appeared in the suggestions put by the main print unions to Rupert Murdoch's News International in response to his demand for a legally binding no-strike agreement to cover his newspaper-printing plant at Wapping, east London.

The other was to be found in the draft agreement put forward, with the full support of the TUC, by the Civil Service unions to cover staff at GCHQ after the Government announced its ban on trade unions there. Though the unions were careful to stress that what they were offering was not a no-strike agreement but a no-disruption agreement, it was hard to see how in practice the distinction would have been maintained. The draft proposal stated:

> It is agreed that there shall be included in the conditions of service of staff employed in or under GCHQ a provision that they will take no action which would or might interfere with the uninterrupted operation of essential security services. To provide for the immunity from risk of industrial disruption whether in pursuit of national or local disputes . . . the trade union side will not instruct or ask members employed in or under GCHQ to take any action which might put at risk the continuous maintenance, twenty-four hours a day, seven days a week, of essential security and intelligence services at GCHQ.[65]

The Prime Minister rejected the offer as insufficient – 'with a disdain', as Alistair Graham, then moderate general secretary of the civil servants' union CPSA phrased it, 'that portrayed a deep strain of anti-unionism'.

If Mrs Thatcher rejected the concept of a deal which sharply restricted the likelihood of strikes, not so the Liberal–SDP Alliance in relation to the strike-free deals of the electricians and other unions. Ian Wrigglesworth, SDP economic affairs spokesman, told a TUC Congress fringe meeting in 1985 that the Alliance would like to see such agreements statutorily underpinned. Dr David Owen, the SDP's leader, spelt out the Party's philosophy more deeply in his Redcliffe-Maud lecture a few months earlier, arguing strongly for more widespread use of pendulum arbitration as a means of resolving disputes in the private sector, and suggesting a fixed pay-comparability formula, with no provision for bargaining, for certain public sector groups such as teachers, social workers and emergency service employees who would have to settle in return for a no-strike agreement.

The new, strike-free deals virtually all contain specific references ruling out strikes, or other industrial action, while the procedure provided for in the agreement – most often leading to pendulum arbitration – is in force. At Hitachi, for instance, the agreement states:

> The company and the EETPU have agreed that all conflicts of interest between the company and its Members will be resolved without lock-out and without any form of industrial action by any individual or any group of company Members.

Inmos' deal agrees the need to 'avoid any action which interrupts the continuity of production', though it is further reinforced in a jointly issued Inmos–EETPU statement of February 1983, which says, 'there is explicit understanding that the agreement provides alternative methods for resolving' issues other than 'the traditional recourse to industrial action of any kind'. Optical Fibres takes a similar line, pledging both sides to 'avoid any action which interrupts the continuity of production', as does Xidex (formerly Control Data): 'A fundamental understanding is that during any phase of this new procedure, all normal working practices are observed and maintained.' Sanyo's agreement 'precludes the necessity for recourse to any form of industrial action', while Toshiba's 'provides for the resolution of conflicts of interest between the company and its employees through consultation, negotiation and arbitration rather than the traditional processes of industrial action'. Nissan's agreement with the AUEW states: 'There will be no industrial action of any kind while an issue is in procedure, or the subject of conciliation or arbitration.' Finally, NEK Cables' deal with the GMBATU precludes involvement in any industrial action called for from outside the company, and says:

> It is specifically agreed that no strikes, lockouts, slowdown, stoppage of work or departure from normal working practices or any other form of industrial action whether by the company, the union, or the employees will take place whilst the grievance, dispute or difference is being investigated either in the domestic situation or in the stages of procedure.

Balance in the Strike-Free Package

Like all agreements, the strike-free package reaches for a balance, with most of the elements within it cutting at least two ways: single unionism, for instance, is clearly of benefit to both union and management. The union obtains sole bargaining rights (so, at least potentially, increasing its power, influence, membership, even its prospects for survival and growth); the company is able to simplify and concentrate its industrial relations and personnel efforts, without having the duplication which multi-unionism makes inevitable. Union critics of the strike-free deals attack them precisely because they see them as unbalanced. Larry Brooke, national electronics officer of Tass, the engineering union, sees the EETPU package as a sham, which will not stand scrutiny – in the main because, in agreeing to limit strikes, it hands up too much power to the employer, it pushes the balance too far one way. Looking at how the elements of the package interrelate – single-unionism makes flexibility easier, demarcation lines can best be eased if there are no overt differences in employees' terms and conditions, for instance – it is difficult to accept agreement, even if one believes that the strike weapon is single-edged, that it does not cut the employee as much as the employer. As Eric Hammond, EETPU general secretary, puts it: 'Our critics dwell on this aspect as if they think strikes are an end in themselves.' Currently, with the overall balance of industrial relations power very much in the employers' favour, the much more equal poise of the strike-free deals may look almost anomalous. But the balance can tilt the other way, if the unions were to experience a resurgence of their power of the 1960s and 1970s. The package was born at Toshiba's plant in Plymouth. How has it fared there?

7

Strike Free: The Testbed

Joan Griffiths walks down the factory's production line – a nod here, a greeting there, stopping to point out a tiny deviation in quality, complaining with pride and satisfaction that one of the company's key products is so much in demand that staff at the plant cannot even buy one for themselves. A production manager? A managing director? Far, far from it. 'The arrogance has gone from management now,' she says. 'They are part of this agreement too.'

Joan Griffiths is the EETPU's senior shop steward at Toshiba, the Japanese-owned television manufacturer in Plymouth, tucked virtually under the Tamar road bridge which speeds thousands of holidaymakers on their way to Cornwall's coves and beaches. In 1981, Toshiba became the first company to feature the strike-free package in practice. The testbed of the idea, it has since become almost a social laboratory, peered at by teams of delicately probing industrial relations experts. 'On the shop floor,' she says, 'we feel we are in a goldfish bowl, we get so many visitors.' Popular, expansive, every inch a Devonian, she marshals the tours round the factory, the company's personnel people studiously dropping back. She is the agreement's best advertisement: 'People are still not believing that our system can work. We're sick to death of telling people that it *does* work.' But she is hardly promulgating a glowing, copywriter's whitewash: 'Let's not fool ourselves,' she says. 'I'm not going to be that naive to say that it's all wonderful. Of course there are times when I think that management are totally wrong. We are bound to have problems. But it's not the fact that we get problems – it's how we try to deal with them.' Her refusal to accept Toshiba's system uncritically only goes to reinforce the genuineness of her enthusiasm for it.

Toshiba's Plymouth plant provides the best opportunity to test how the grand theory of the strike-free deal works out in hard reality. Much of the package was worked out at Toshiba; much of the thinking through of its features happened there, as Roy Sanderson says:

> I met the British management of Toshiba and agreed with them that we would get a blank sheet of paper, and on it we would try to identify the cause of industrial conflict in Britain. We reasoned that if we could identify the causes, we ought to be able to develop an agreement that if not eliminating them, would at least reduce them to a minimum. That was the method we chose – quite simple. And that's how we did it.

Simple enough it sounds – though quite extraordinary for the tangled web of British industrial relations, particularly at a time of recession when many managements, far from sitting down with their unions to try to eliminate the causes of conflict, were seizing the opportunity of union weakness to leap into the industrial relations driving-seat, and showing every sign of finding life at the wheel quite exhilarating. Almost as extraordinary, perhaps, was that this was being done not at a time of reasoned, placid calm – but at the very moment of acute industrial crisis, when Rank-Toshiba collapsed, and thousands of its employees were thrown on to the dole.

Bush Radio, started in 1932 by four employees of a failed radio company, was brought into the Rank Organisation during the second world war, though it retained its own identity. Based in Chiswick, west London, its expansion forced it to start looking for a second production site, and in June 1947 work started on a factory at Ernesettle, on Plymouth's northern outskirts. The company was expanding with the booming television market. Rank Radio International was formed in 1972, drawing together under one heading a rash of consumer electronics companies – among them Bush, Leak, Murphy, Wharfedale and Dansette. The following year was the company's peak: £87 million turnover, £8 million profits. The Plymouth factory had 3700 employees.

Then the oil crisis hit, and the television industry began spiralling downward. By the end of the 1970s, Rank's losses were being stemmed. But it was clearly far from ungrateful when Toshiba, now the world's ninth-largest electronic equipment company – 'Expertise, enthusiasm, idealism, commitment' runs the slogan on the map in the hall of Plymouth Toshiba – approached Rank, keen like other Japanese enterprises to gain a manufacturing foothold within the EEC. Toshiba had been supplying cathode tubes to Rank for its TV sets for some time, so the connection was there: the formation of Rank-Toshiba on 1 November 1978 forged it in steel, and brought considerable relief to employees worried for their job security.

Or so it seemed. Those involved in the joint venture now admit privately that little was in fact done to turn round the plant's fortunes. On 26 September 1980, the two companies announced that the partnership was to be ended. Rank offered its 70 per cent shareholding to Toshiba; Toshiba not only declined the offer, but offered its 30 per cent to Rank. A deal was eventually struck: Rank would buy Toshiba's shares for a 'nominal consideration', on condition that Toshiba took over the main Plymouth plant (Rank's second West Country plant, at Redruth in Cornwall, closed down completely) and employed as many as possible of the existing workforce. The Ernesettle plant closed on 20 March 1981.

Plymouth, where the company was a major employer second only to the shaky naval dockyard, was devastated. Wyn Bevan, the EETPU's executive councillor for the area, is unequivocal: 'One of the most traumatic redundancies of the period'. Some 2600 employees lost their jobs. Sanderson was the EETPU officer whose task it was to negotiate the deal. He fought the closure as hard as he could, even travelling to Japan with Dr David Owen, the local MP who was just crossing the Labour rubicon to form the SDP, to plead the plant's case with Toshiba's worldwide president, Shoichi Saba. Back in Plymouth, Sanderson and Geoffrey Deith, the joint venture's managing director, and managing director of the new company, Toshiba Consumer Products (UK), which was to operate the Plymouth plant, worked fast. Putting together their own ideas, selling them first to Kenichiro Hiyama, chairman of the company and of Toshiba UK (the multinational's UK marketing arm, formed in 1973), and then from him on to Japan, they hammered out the strike-free deal. By the time TCP officially began life, on 2 April, the EETPU was able to announce its new deal on the same day, featuring 'some of the best industrial relations practices to be found anywhere in British industry, and some that are quite new and that point the way for the future'.[1] The new arrangements had their first test when the company started up with just 280 employees on 4 May: a bank holiday – but there was no mention, no thought probably, of extra payment for working it.

Though the EETPU was what seems in retrospect surprisingly modest about emphasising the agreement, and in particular its strike-free provisions, at the time the deal seemed – indeed, still seems – extraordinary: overnight, six of the plant's seven unions gone, new ways of working, new standards, new industrial relations – a single union, single status, no demarcation, full employee involvement in decision-making, disputes resolved by binding, pendulum arbitration, and no strikes.

Five years and more later, how does it seem? How has it worked? Is it accepted? 'We have our doubters and cynics,' says George Harris, Toshiba's personnel manager. Some staff, for instance, 'constantly search for problems and issues to raise. But they are a small minority who, perhaps a little generously, my managing director regards as the "conscience" of the company.' By most measurable standards, it *has* worked: employment has risen to about 900, three times the original starting complement; a vast range of new TV models has been brought in, with more constantly being introduced; the company has moved in to assembling video recorders; and a new, 9000 square-metre factory has been established at Belliver, four miles away, making microwave ovens, and was opened by Dr Owen just over four years after fighting the original plant's closure. Production is now rising fast: 265,000 colour television sets (including the 14-inch remote, which even the staff find it hard to get their hands on) in 1985–6, compared to 145,000 in 1983–4; 110,000 video recorders in the same year, compared to 93,000 in 1984–5, and none at all the previous year.

Employees at Toshiba testify that they are glad to be working there, that it is a good – though strict – company for which to work. Pay has risen well, too: 5 per cent increases in 1985, 7 per cent the year before, 7.5 per cent the year before that.[2] In 1983, the company introduced a dividend scheme for all employees (other than company directors), which is triggered if bottom-line profits rise above a certain agreed level, with 75 per cent of the extra profit going into the dividend. Its first year of operation saw all employees receive a lump sum from it: £100 per person per half year.

In the main, the industrial relations contribution to the company's overall performance has worked well: problems are dealt with at the company advisory board, members meeting in their blue uniform jackets at a round teak table in a coolly painted ground-floor room. But problems there have been, as the system has bedded down.

None has warranted triggering the pendulum arbitration provision, nor gone near it. But all are significant indications of the workings in practice of the strike-free agreements.

Growth

Des Thomson, Toshiba's managing director, sits at a desk in the large, open-plan office he and all the other managerial, administrative and clerical staff share at the plant. Arriving at Toshiba in 1982 from the hurly-burly of British Leyland, he wondered what he was doing there. 'It seemed to me a company that had everything perfectly organised.' Quickly, he found that that was not quite the case: 'It was operating at 50 per cent of capacity, with a model range of eight. In 1985 alone we are introducing thirty-two new models.' Thomson is pleased, and proud of the company's growth, but accepts that it is not without its difficulties: 'The concepts on which we started are all still intact, but some of the essential attitudes of people who became the first group of employees within the company have clearly now been very diluted.' Of Toshiba's first 280 employees, Thomson reckons about 20 per cent have now gone through wastage of various kinds. 'They had been part of a large, traditional UK company – and they had seen that company fold, something they never imagined would happen. They saw themselves with no real job prospects in this area.' Given the opportunity of joining a new company, their level of commitment to, motivation by and understanding of what was being done at Toshiba was very high: they had gone through the fire.

Now, though, the jobshock of the Rank closure seems, even for those who endured it, far away. That has been heightened by the employees the company has taken on since. 'An awful lot of people who now work for the company didn't go through that common, shared experience,' says Thomson. 'Some of them start here from school. They walk in and find all this, a very open industrial society. And they say, so what? Isn't industry all like this?' That lack of understanding has led to a change, perhaps even a diffusion, in the company's culture. Some managers there feel the change pointedly: 'When the original people talk about "our company",' said one manager, 'they really mean our company. When some of the new people talk about "our company", it often just means the place where we work.' Thomson thinks the optimum number on a site which would allow an industrial relations system like Toshiba's to work properly is about 700, roughly the current scale of the television plant. Further growth may shift the balance inside the plant still further.

Agreement Principles

That form of change has helped bring about other, less intangible alterations to the plant's way of working, and in particular to the operation of the agreement and the principles lying behind it. Take flexibility as an example. In many areas, flexibility is fully in practice, though in others employees report that they would prefer a change of work within the plant. The company has knowingly moved away from the concept of complete flexibility in an important area. 'Sub-keys' in Toshiba – roughly, though not exactly, equivalent to a leading hand in a normal engineering factory – used to be appointed by the management solely, but the jobs are now open to application by operators. It is a step up in responsibility and authority (pay, too). But operators thinking of applying were being dissuaded: if they were given the new job, not only would they have to perform all that it required, but they might easily, under the flexibility provisions, have to do it in a wholly new section of the plant. So the CoAB (company advisory board) decided that all new sub-keys should remain in their own occupational sections for at least a year, and moved after that only for good, agreed reasons. 'We have walked away from flexibility in this area,' says Thomson, 'but we've done so for sound practical reasons.'

A similar pragmatism governed another shift. As part of the agreement's single-status provisions, all employees were to be paid monthly, in practice by bank credit transfer. But after a couple of years, complaints began to come through that some were finding it difficult to budget in this way; could they not return to weekly wages? The management pointed out that common terms and conditions were a fundamental part of the concept underlying the agreement, and that meant monthly pay. All right, came the reply, could we not be paid in 13 equal amounts, once every four weeks, so that we would know where we were? Managers said no: Toshiba operates monthly accounts world-wide – that has to remain. To settle it, the company balloted the workforce, but the results were inconclusive, divided roughly evenly between those wanting to revert, those actively against it, and those to whom it was immaterial. The industrial relations system in the plant is wholly designed to allow both sides to find a way forward together, but on this, they were unable to. 'There was conflict,' says Thomson. 'Not enough to go to pendulum arbitration – but there was conflict.' In the end, a compromise was reached: all staff now have a mid-monthly payment put into their bank accounts (a system since adopted elsewhere, for example at Hitachi). 'It had been a Mexican standoff,' Thomson says, 'but we managed it.'

CoAB

In that case, CoAB accepted the compromise virtually as soon as it heard of it. But not all the advisory board's workings have run so smoothly. Some managers found its operation difficult to accept: often, its meetings would run into the evening, with decisions being taken at them which managers would only hear about the next morning, often after the unofficial grapevine and official post-CoAB report back systems had already informed everyone else. Managers are now allowed to observe the meetings, and may be told the same evening of key developments.

Some CoAB members found it difficult to comprehend the mass of detailed financial information regularly provided by the company (the union members on CoAB supplement this with research material supplied from the EETPU's head office). The company introduced special evening seminars for CoAB members and any other interested employees on balance-sheet reading, and explaining the work in detail of different departments so that their performance could be understood. Reports back have changed, too; the company tried to bring in a video system, getting board members to record their reports quickly for distribution within the plant, but found that the necessary speed allowed no time for polishing video performances, leaving them wooden and uninspiring. The idea was abandoned, reverting to the normal oral reports, supported by joint statements and then publication of the full minutes.

Board members admit, as well, that many of the workforce are still shy of the system – and that shows in the elections to the board itself. The company tries hard to stimulate interest both in the elections and in standing for election. Personnel staff now prepare short manifestos, with photographs, of candidates standing. The company clearly likes to see a turnover on the board – not so that workforce representatives are constantly less expert in dealing with the information presented to them, but to maintain interest, to sustain representativeness, and to prevent signs of a drift towards the board being composed of mainly higher-grade employees. The relationship of the union to the board has also had its difficulties. Because only the senior steward is on the board by right, there have been conflicts of authority between CoAB representatives and stewards in the same work area – especially at times of pay discussions. The company has discerned a noticeable, though not easily definable, difference between employees wanting to become stewards and those wanting to become CoAB members; it is keen for the standards of both to be similar, to prevent any frictions developing.

Trade Unionism

Strong criticism is always levelled against the EETPU and other unions signing strike-free and single-union deals that their sole purpose is to increase the union's membership. If that is the case, then the strategy is singularly failing at Toshiba, the progenitor of all the deals which followed. There is no closed shop at Toshiba, in line with EETPU thinking. Union membership has fluctuated, but has remained roughly constant, at around 50 per cent. There are members of other unions in the plant – both Apex and ASTMS in the clerical areas, for instance – but there were more: many have let their membership lapse, some are non-union, others go to the EETPU with their problems. 'In a company like this the trade union is more valuable than in a normal company,' says Joan Griffiths. 'Our management are supposed to be so clever, and so agreeable – but it doesn't always work like that.'

Towards the end of 1985, the company and the union agreed on a special recruiting drive: the EETPU set up a special display in the plant, trying to draw people into the union. Now, too, as part of the induction process, all new employees meet Joan Griffiths, who explains to them the benefits of EETPU membership, and asks them to sign up; there is a success rate in this of more than 90 per cent. As a result, union membership among the employees – two-thirds women, with an average age across the company of about twenty-six – has risen to about 75 per cent; higher than it has been, but still a long way from the membership grab which many of the EETPU's detractors see lurking behind the strike-free deals. 'I don't want the EETPU to become a minority voice in the organisation,' says Des Thomson – an astonishing enough admission that such a thought could even be entertained at Toshiba, of all plants, often seen as the jewel in the electricians' crown. He regards the union as part of the philosophy and approach of the company; he has considerable respect for the union's officials inside the plant, and for Sanderson and Eric Hammond, who attended the opening of the company's second factory. Thomson is also being pragmatic, because if the EETPU did become a 'small force' in the company, another union might start pressing for recognition.

It is hard to see the EETPU declining so far. Both the union and the company have achieved a considerable amount at Toshiba. Between them, they have turned round the company's fortunes, taken on more people, brought in new products; and they have not lost a day's production through strikes or other industrial action. In those respects, the Toshiba experience *does* seem to bear out the promise of the original agreement, and so offers support to all similar agreements. But the company is still young: Shoichi Saba, the Toshiba Corporation's president, says of Plymouth that, having been born in 1981, it has now reached adolescence. Des Thomson agrees: 'As an adolescent we are becoming capable of doing an awful lot of things for ourselves, but we're still learning to grow up and understand the world we're in.' With unemployment still high in the area, employees at the plant measure things more simply, looking at survival, never mind expansion, as a step forward. 'When we started in Toshiba there were only 300 people,' says Joan Griffiths. 'We are now nearly 1000. If that's a backward step, please tell me why.'

8

Strike Free: The Deals Spread

In the wake of the Toshiba agreement, the strike-free deals started to spread – slowly, certainly, and sticking in the main to the electronics industry. The radical ideas promulgated in Plymouth had caught both the attention and the practical intention of other companies, and other unions. Most of the new deals provided in practice the changed climate and harmonious relations which they had promised in theory. After the crises in which many were born, they offered security: 'The best thing about this factory now,' said a shop steward in one plant covered by a strike-free deal, 'is that you feel safe enough to go away on holiday.'

Many of the new agreements, too, were an improvement on the first. Not just in terms of learning from it, and fine-tuning its industrial relations provisions and practices, but in the benefits they offered. Wyn Bevan, who negotiated the Hitachi deal for the electricians' union, claims that it is in this area by far the best the union has yet done – it provides a job security guarantee, for instance, and benefits markedly better than others in industry. For bereavements, for instance, the company's final working agreement[1] provides for up to five days' paid leave for a death in the immediate family (defined as father, mother, husband, wife, son, daughter, brother, sister, grandmother or grandfather) – in sharp contrast to some practices elsewhere, such as the proposals tabled at the end of 1985 by the American-owned brake company Clayton Dewandre as part of a single-union (with the AUEW) package for employees at its Lincoln plant, which stipulate that absenteeism for family bereavement will lead to summary dismissal unless a death certificate can be produced.[2]

But the deals after Toshiba also brought with them difficulties, especially in two areas – single unionism and the resolution of disputes – which carried implications for the agreements themselves, and for the unions and employees covered by them, affecting wider issues beyond the boundaries of the factories concerned.

Single Unionism: Hitachi

Ten miles from the South Wales mining village of Maerdy, where the 1984–5 coal strike ended at its most emotional, men who had stayed out solidly for a year marching back to their pit behind a brass band, lies the little town of Hirwaun. Just outside it, on a small industrial estate guarded by cattle-grids, nestling behind a Dunlopillo factory, lies the Hitachi television and video manufacturing plant. 'This factory used to be awful,' says Wyn Bevan, EETPU executive councillor for the area. 'Discipline was non-existent – people strolling off the production lines to do whatever they wanted to, whenever they wanted. The lines were full of pies, and pasties and cups of tea, people smoking and tapping ash. You can't have sophisticated electronic equipment with pieces of pasty and cups of tea falling all over it.' Now, it no longer does. Once a cornerstone in the growth of the giant GEC company – Lord Weinstock, its managing director, was once managing director of the Hirwaun plant for a year, and married the daughter of its founder, Sir Michael Sobell – the plant, like Toshiba, was run as a joint venture with GEC for five years, before GEC pulled out in 1984. 'The joint venture period was horrendous,' says one senior Hitachi executive now. 'What looked like a sensible business decision was really just an expedient business decision.' Hitachi resolved the problem by facing the company with a choice, as it spelt out to its workforce:

> In plain financial terms, the existing business at Hirwaun is bankrupt. In blunt assessment terms, the existing factory standards and efficiencies are the worst in the UK in any competitor comparison. Hitachi has recently considered two options:
> (1.1) Withdraw from Hirwaun because it will be impossible to change the business to profitability within reasonable timescales.
> (1.2) Take control of the business and install Hitachi conditions and standards as quickly as possible, because this will give potential to change the business to profitability within reasonable timescales.
> The Hitachi decision has, of course, already been made.[3]

That decision was wholly to recast the plant's fabric and operations, to reduce sharply its workforce, and to reach a radical labour relations agreement on the lines of the Toshiba deal: in short, to start a new, greenfield factory on the site of and in the shell of an old, traditional plant. It was a decision which was to prove successful for the company, which has managed to move from loss-making towards profitability. It was also a decision which was to embody long-term implications for the EETPU and for the structure of British trade unionism. Acas officials warned at the time in an internal paper of the possibility of union recognition 'sparking off the majority of industrial relations problems so far' with the strike-free deals, and suggested that such moves 'can provoke substantial disruption to industrial relations within the companies concerned, and employers will need to consider carefully the problems that any change in long-standing agreements can provoke, and balance them against expected benefits.'[4]

They were right. In the days of the joint GEC-Hitachi venture, there were a number of unions recognised at the plant – the EETPU (716 members), AUEW (223), ASTMS (87), Ucatt (87), Apex (60) and Tass (15). In addition, the TGWU (10) had unofficial 'representational' rights, and there were 115 non-union employees.[5] As part of its new agreement, Hitachi was insistent on recognising only one union. It chose the EETPU, its largest – though, as one manager now puts it: 'I must say that we felt rather fortunate that the majority union *was* the EETPU.'

In April 1984, the company wrote to its unions, informing them that it planned to announce a single-union deal with the EETPU at the end of the month. Outraged, the other unions sought immediate meetings with the company, and then with the TUC, to complain about the EETPU's behaviour. Hitachi on 30 April served formal notice on the five recognised unions other than the EETPU that it would withdraw their recognition with effect from 14 May. Four days before that date, at a testy meeting, the EETPU refused to join the other unions in a common approach to the company. The other unions decided to press a formal complaint against the electricians under the TUC's Bridlington principles governing inter-union relations, while the company delayed its withdrawal of recognition until 10 August – the day before the formal opening of its single-union agreement with the EETPU.

The stage was now set. The TUC, on 5 June, tried informally to bring together the EETPU and the other six unions – the TGWU, though not recognised, had joined the complaint. It was a failure. A disputes committee, headed by Jack Eccles, from GMBATU, that year's TUC chairman, and with Eric Nevin, general secretary of the merchant navy officers' union, and John Scott-Garner, president of the then-Post Office Engineering Union, met on 24 July to hear, and reject, the EETPU's claim that it had no case to answer. A final attempt at the meeting to reconcile the two sides again failed.

While the TUC's machinery ground slowly on, the pace of change at local level was accelerating. At the end of April, the company began a lengthy process of explaining to its employees what the changes, spelt out in a document called 'A New Future at Hirwaun', would mean. Employees were seen in groups of thirty-five, and each received a copy of the paper, explaining the new deal: 508 redundancies, a 7 per cent pay increase, single status, full flexibility, a company members' board, pendulum arbitration, no strikes – and a single union. Ann Clwyd, Labour MP for Cynon Valley, formally and publicly protested at the redundancies, but Wyn Bevan got down to the task of negotiations on them, and on the agreement.

Bevan says now that the talks on the agreement, bringing it down from what he describes as the company's original 'draconian' proposals, were among the hardest he has ever known. Convinced himself, he began the uphill task of first convincing the EETPU's shop stewards, and then the union's members – as the company had done, meeting them in small groups, painstakingly going over and over every small point of the detailed, thirty-three-page document. For the employees, single unionism was not an issue, according to Tony Pegge, Hitachi's personnel executive:

> Most of the company members in the factory didn't know which union they were a member of. They *were* concerned about being union members, but not concerned about the single-union matter. Single-union matters were problems for full-time officials.

Problems there were for the unions. On 16 June, in the cinema in nearby Aberdare, the six unions held a mass meeting – at which, it was claimed, 550 Hitachi employees, including 100 EETPU members, were present – and it voted unanimously against signing the agreement. A month later, those being made redundant had gone, and the EETPU, negotiations concluded, organised a secret ballot of its remaining members in the company on the 'New Future' document. The result was overwhelming: 87 per cent in favour. The union and the company signed the agreement the same day. It came into effect on 8 August – and by the end of the week, the other unions were out.

Seething, frustrated, all that the other unions had left now was the hope that the TUC would rule the agreement out of order (though the company was making it abundantly clear that what the TUC did or said did not concern it, or its agreement with the EETPU). With all urgency gone, and the TUC finally beginning to become involved in the miners' strike, the full disputes committee hearing was not held until 16 January. Led by Tim Webb, from ASTMS, for the six unions, and Bevan and Roy Sanderson for the EETPU, the two sides locked horns in the TUC's headquarters, Congress House, in London's Bloomsbury. TUC disputes committee findings, let alone the hearings, are confidential, but a seventeen-page internal TUC report of what the TUC described with considerable understatement as a 'difficult dispute' makes plain what occurred.[6]

The six unions' charge was straightforward enough. The EETPU had signed a single-union deal with Hitachi. The other recognised unions had been excluded. The EETPU was therefore in breach – on two counts – of Bridlington. As the TUC report says: 'It was the complainant unions' view that they had been faced throughout with collaboration between an affiliated trade union and an employer in an attempt to destroy the then-current and long-standing organisational negotiating rights of other union members.'

The EETPU rejected that claim. Bevan and Sanderson said that they had not tried to poach other unions' members, and gave an undertaking that they would not do so. In effect, Hitachi presented a wholly new employment position; in so far as the TUC's Bridlington principles applied, they had complied with them. They had been faced with an intransigent employer: 'To have pursued the action suggested by the complainant unions and refused to enter into a single-union agreement would, in the EETPU's view, have led Hitachi to withdraw recognition from all unions and establish a non-union plant.'

Hitachi, then, crystallised a crucial part of the EETPU's whole argument in favour of its strike-free package: that, or nothing – no unions at all. Eric Hammond made it clear, too, that the EETPU would rather face possible expulsion from the TUC for refusing to accept the disputes' committee award, if it went against the union, than abandon its deal at Hitachi and the principles it represented. In the event, he did not have to go that far. On 11 April, the TUC made its ruling known to the unions concerned. The EETPU had a sharp ruler across its knuckles: 'The EETPU should not have signed the sole recognition and negotiating agreement until the dispute had been resolved, if necessary by TUC adjudication.' But it was not ordered to abandon the deal. Instead, it had to meet three points: new employees at Hitachi should be advised that they might join a union other than the EETPU; in the case of grievances at the plant involving a member of one of the ousted unions, an official of the union concerned should be able to take the issue up with the company; and the EETPU should establish a body which would allow the ousted unions to relay to the company through the electricians their views on issues affecting them.

TUC disputes committee awards are binding, and Hammond immediately welcomed the ruling as a vindication of the EETPU's stance. Webb was appalled – so appalled that, on behalf of the ousted unions, he took a step unprecedented in the TUC and tried to appeal against the committee's decision. He challenged each of the three stipulations, arguing in particular that the second was impracticable, since officials from unions other than the EETPU were now no longer allowed on to Hitachi premises at Hirwaun. Of the third, Webb said in a letter to Norman Willis, TUC general secretary: 'The establishment of a body whereby the previously recognised unions submit their views to the EETPU who then consider them before presenting a claim to the employer, must be a potentially unique institution in joint trade union procedures. It is difficult to see how this could work.'[7] But it was not, in any case, the central issue. 'The overall problem is, of course, that six unions with legitimate and long-standing negotiating rights have had these removed by an agreement between the employer and another trade union. The disputes committee award does not redress this situation.' But Willis was adamantine: 'There is no appeal against an award of a TUC disputes committee.'[8] So the EETPU had won the first round – but a month later, battle was joined again when Apex, one of the six ousted unions, successfully pressed the TUC at its annual Congress to tighten its regulations on single-union deals.

Hitachi brought out into the open what Acas has called the 'cut-throat' fight for membership[9] as union numbers tighten and the prospect of membership gains in areas like the high-technology industries seems to beckon invitingly. But, along with the EETPU's strike-free deal with Eddie Shah's *Today* newspaper, it effectively brought about the TUC's ban on unions' unilateral signing of single-union deals. The EETPU (and others who would take this course if they could) has staked a considerable part of its philosophy and future on just such agreements; it may yet be that complying with the TUC's alterations to Bridlington may prove too high a price for the EETPU to pay for continued membership of the TUC.

Dispute Resolution

Sanyo

Sanyo's strike-free agreement with the EETPU, like those at Toshiba and Hitachi, was born out of crisis. In October 1980, Philips announced the closure of its television plant at Lowestoft, in Suffolk, because of overcapacity in the industry. The company wanted to concentrate its manufacturing in Croydon, Surrey; 1100 lost their jobs at Lowestoft. Like many Japanese companies, Sanyo was looking for a manufacturing base inside the EEC. 'We were approached by Sanyo,' says Noel Salmon, then with Philips, now Sanyo's head of personnel, 'who bought the site. They didn't want the people, just the site.' To run the new plant, Sanyo signed back on about 250 of those formerly employed with Philips (though on lower rates of pay), and, after looking at Toshiba, reached a single-union, strike-free agreement with the EETPU in June 1982, which provided for differences to be resolved by pendulum arbitration, if necessary, and stipulated against industrial action. Those reprieved, who made up the new workforce, were in no doubt about the extent of the change, according to Rod Cooper, EETPU senior steward: 'People have come to realise that the whole situation is totally different. The boot's on the other foot, if you like – and that's accepted.'[10]

That level of acceptance was a contributory factor to three successfully concluded sets of annual pay negotiations. But by December 1984, the lower pay levels at Sanyo were causing the union difficulty. Partly, it was an unseen clash between two planes of the labour market: geographically, rates at Sanyo were in line with the market rates in low-paid East Anglia; within the industry, the EETPU calculated that Sanyo's process workers, for instance, received about £18 a week less than the average, and other employers were starting to quote Sanyo against the EETPU when seeking increases elsewhere, arguing that if the union could sanction such pay levels at Sanyo, why not elsewhere? Roy Sanderson, the EETPU's national officer with responsibility for the electronics industry, and the union were determined to try to improve Sanyo pay levels.

Accordingly, the union tabled a claim within the company's joint negotiating council, for a flat-rate weekly increase of £15, plus reduced hours and improved holidays; the company replied with an offer of 6 per cent plus at first one week's and later two weeks' extra bonus payment. The offer was rejected in a ballot of the workforce. Under Sanyo procedure, Sanderson at this point stepped into the negotiations, and on 13 December, the union tabled a claim aimed at making up over three years what it saw as the pay shortfall – 30 per cent in the first year, 50 per cent in the second, and full parity in the third. At this point, accounts of events between the company and the union start to conflict sharply – creating at the time a considerable degree of at least misunderstanding, and at worst a good deal more than that. EETPU members now say that the company was at the time doing nothing to rebut rumours in the plant that the union's claim was for an increase of £12 a week, since the company felt that to go to pendulum arbitration with such a claim from the union would inevitably lead to a finding in the company's favour. Sanderson now acknowledges he did use such a figure in the negotiations, but only as an illustrative point, not as a definitive claim. The company replied by improving its offer, giving a further week's bonus and an extra day's annual holiday entitlement. The offer was again rejected in a workforce ballot, and the issue was jointly referred to arbitration.

The two sides asked Acas to provide an arbitrator. Acas keeps a list of arbitrators for deployment in disputes, and from it the service suggested Professor Sid Kessler, an industrial relations academic from the City University, London, with extensive arbitration experience. On 2 January, the two sides agreed terms of reference for Kessler, which were:

(1) To attempt to resolve the disagreement between Sanyo and the EETPU over the review of salaries and conditions of employment due on 1 December 1984.
(2) In the event that a mediated settlement is not possible, then to arbitrate a settlement by deciding for the company's case only, or, the union's case only.

The significant point about these terms of reference, confirmed by letter to Acas, is that mediation – a non-binding award by a third party – is not written into the company's strike-free deal with the

EETPU. Why both sides went outside the agreement seems to have again been a difference of understanding, in this case of what exactly mediation was. Fact-finding plays a considerable part in US pendulum arbitration deals – a point of which Sanderson was unaware when he negotiated first Toshiba's and then Sanyo's agreements: 'At the time that those agreements were made, I was not aware of the refinements that had taken place to straightforward final-offer arbitration.' Sanderson sees the whole point of pendulum arbitration as being a device to keep people in procedure, to keep them negotiating, until a deal is reached, and so was impressed by the flexibility a further, inserted, stage seemed to offer. Sanyo either did not fully realise that these were Sanderson's intentions, or simply saw the mediation mechanism provided for in the terms of reference as a short staging-post on the way to pendulum arbitration.

Kessler arrived in Lowestoft on 9 January, and was presented with both sides' statement of case in preparation for the hearing the following day. Both sides also exchanged their statements. To the surprise of both Kessler and Noel Salmon, heading Sanyo's team, the EETPU appeared to have changed its offer. Its written claim in its final statement of case was no longer for a three-year deal, but for three points, on top of the company's final offer: an increase of £1.86 per week on all salaries from 1 December 1984; a thirty-nine-hour working week from 1 July, 1985; and an extra day's holiday from January 1986, with a further day in January 1987. Salmon was appalled – given what he thought was the union's claim, he was convinced the company would be successful if that and the company's were tested by pendulum arbitration; he therefore had been ready to take that step, confident the company would not be faced with the cost of meeting the union's whole claim. For his part, Sanderson denies strongly that there was any change of claim, insisting that the union had only ever wanted to move towards its target of parity for Sanyo pay with outside comparable companies in stages, and that this was simply the first stage for the year under review. But, in any case, he contends that under the American experience of pendulum arbitration which he was taking as his model, altering the claim right up to the final moment is perfectly permissible.

Kessler opened the hearing on 10 January. Salmon protested at what he saw as the union's changed claim, insisting in a statement that 'the integrity of pendulum arbitration entirely depends upon both parties declaring their final position for consideration at the final negotiating discussions.' He said: 'The concept behind pendulum arbitration is, we believe, to make negotiators carefully consider the content and direction of their final negotiating position in the knowledge that, without agreement, those positions would be tested by arbitration. Changes made at the arbitration stage are not in keeping with the concept behind the pendulum arbitration process.' Salmon asked Kessler to rule on which was the union's final claim. Kessler, while sympathising in principle with the company, found in favour of the union's written claim, submitted the night before.

Sanderson was now surprised when the company then challenged the terms of reference, arguing against mediation and in favour of the procedure as contained in its written agreement with the union. Though the agreement makes provision for pendulum arbitration, it is not wholly mandatory, and Salmon looked likely now to refuse to proceed to that stage. Though he saw a conflict of interest in the two roles, Kessler told both sides that under mediation, as he saw it, he would make recommendations and allow the two sides to consider them, before proceeding further. The company and the union eventually agreed to this. Kessler considered, and came back with a compromise proposal – a 7 per cent pay increase; three weeks' bonus for 1984, to be paid by the end of January 1985; an extra day's holiday from January 1985, and a further day twelve months later; and a thirty-nine-hour working week, without loss of pay, from 1 December 1985.

Sanyo accepted Kessler's suggestion that night. The EETPU asked for time. The union was in fact caught in a ticklish dilemma. If the company accepted the recommendation and the union rejected it, the union felt that Kessler as arbitrator as well as mediator would be likely to find in favour of the company under pendulum arbitration. So by rejecting the mediated offer, the EETPU thought it likely that the union might end up with having to accept a worse offer than that already accepted by the company. As Sanderson puts it now, 'The members would have scorched us.' After anguishing overnight, the hearing reconvened on the morning of 11 January, and the union accepted Kessler's proposal.

But the matter did not end there. Privately, though the company was probably not unhappy with the level of settlement, it was distinctly concerned about the method by which it was reached; in particular, by what it saw as the union's changed claim. Both sides agreed to look at their existing agreement, to try to see if it could be made more specific on what constituted a final position, and how and when arbitration should be triggered. Dennis Boyd, Acas' chief conciliation officer, held a number of meetings with all sides, and eventually the company and union agreed to put to a ballot of Sanyo's workers two separate proposals: the first, supported by the company, that the agreement should remain unchanged; the second, supported by the union, that it should be amended to provide for mediation prior to pendulum arbitration. On 8 May, the workforce voted by 2–1 in favour of maintaining the present agreement.

But, following that vote, the company then drew up a code of practice to clarify how the procedure should operate in any future dispute. The code was essentially twofold. The first element concerned communication:

> Clear communication between the parties is essential to prevent misunderstanding and ambiguity. To this end, the parties will, at all stages of the procedure and before moving from one stage to the next, communicate in writing to each other their proposals for improvements to terms and conditions of employment or for the resolution of the issues under discussion.

At the final negotiating stage, both sides would try to resolve differences by negotiation to the point of putting the issue out to ballot. It was the approach to balloting which provided the second element. Before union ballots, a joint statement would be issued providing a detailed account of each side's position, and facilities would be granted to the union to counsel members on the union's position towards the ballot.

Sanderson now feels that the agreement is clearer for the testing it took; Salmon agrees.

This complicated history of the first real difference under the strike-free deals – Sanyo's 1985 pay settlement sailed through without a hitch – is important because it does show in detail that the operation of the agreements is likely to be more complex in practice than they might seem in theory. In a sense, though activating the procedure was both messy and complicated, it *did* keep people talking, it did produce a settlement to a difficult disagreement without any industrial action. The difficulties surrounding the whole affair perhaps cast the agreements in a poorer light than was warranted, but they raised for arbitrators and industrial relations more generally fundamental questions about the deals' operation. Can the system in practice bear negotiation, conciliation and mediation right up to the point of arbitration? When should negotiations be considered to have broken down? If that point can be determined, should the claim and offer current at that stage be deemed final? Could conciliation at that point, but before pendulum arbitration comes into play, have a role? Despite the company's code of practice, what happened at Sanyo has raised a number of issues which only greater experience of the system will be able to answer.

Bowman Webber

But the strike-free package underwent its greatest test not at one of the plants with showpiece deals, like Nissan or Toshiba, but at a small glass-products manufacturing company in Essex. Tested, too, in two different ways: firstly, there was a strike – the first ever at a company with an agreement designed specifically to prevent them; and secondly, a dispute went right through the procedure, including pendulum arbitration – with the arbitrator, forced to choose between the company's offer and the union's claim, plumping for the union.

Bowman Webber, once a company rooted in London's east end, moved out from Stratford, east London, to Harlow in Essex in January 1985. In London, the predominant union recognised was the Furniture, Timber and Allied Trades Union, FTAT. 'When they moved to Harlow, they gave notice that they would no longer recognise FTAT,' says Ben Rubner, the union's general secretary. 'It was only when the company commenced production at Harlow that it was learned that the EETPU would be the only union that they would recognise. It appears to be quite obvious now that the reason was to secure an agreement containing a strike-free deal.'[11]

In fact, the company had begun talking to the EETPU in October 1984, and by December had signed a deal with the union – virtually the full package: no-strike clause, pendulum arbitration, flexibility, a company consultative committee, a single union. Initially, the atmosphere at the plant was far from harmonious – partly because of the highly strained relations between the EETPU and the FTAT members who kept their cards but who had lost recognition, and partly because the quality and discipline of some of the local labour taken on was poor. But Bowman Webber was expanding, its parent company, the HAT building services group, investing in it £3 million on the expectation of greatly increased profitability: a turnover of £10 million, returning within three–four years an annual profit of about £1 million. But to do that both the company and the EETPU recognised that the plant would have to move from day working to shift work if it was to provide the production capacity required.

The agreement between the company and the union provided for pay rates until the end of February 1986, but twelve months before that the EETPU told the company that industry-wide agreements now put the holiday entitlement up to twenty-one days a year (one more than the Bowman Webber agreement) and a 15-per-cent double day-shift premium. Though the union accepted that it was duty bound to honour the signed agreement with the company, it asked for what it saw as this anomaly to be taken into account. Under the terms of its deal, the company could simply have refused the EETPU's claim, but its managers considered that to do so would be breaking the spirit of the agreement and so agreed to hold discussions with the EETPU before making a move towards shift working, in the hope of achieving a trouble-free transition. In October, the company announced internally its intention to move to shift work; accordingly, the EETPU asked for the promised discussions, since many of its members were concerned that shift work would lead to the end of regular overtime, and so to a possible drop in gross pay.

The union put forward an unspecific original claim, thought to be for a rate of about £160 a week, and eventually a detailed, twelve-point claim was submitted for a rate totalling £176.32, based on claims that moving to shift work would involve a considerable interference with employees' domestic arrangements – especially travelling to and from the plant – and drawing in detailed information about other similar rates in the area and other local labour-market information. The company responded with an offer of an extra £15.03 a week, or 10.7 per cent, arguing that to meet the EETPU's claim in full would cost the company an extra £40,000 a year, bringing into question the viability of continuing some parts of its operations.

The EETPU rejected the offer – a rejection confirmed by a secret ballot. Closely in line with the theory that the prospect of pendulum arbitration brings both sides in negotiations closer together, the union and the company now adjusted their positions. The EETPU cut its complex, twelve-point claim to only three items; introducing a common shift premium regardless of skill or grade rates; bringing in a half-hour per shift paid meal break; and instituting a 40.5 hours payment for those on the proposed 37.5 hours shift duty rota. The company replied with an offer reducing the gross pay put forward in its previous offer, because of reduced hours to be worked, but increased the offered hourly rate. It proposed, too, to apply shift premia to be applied to bonus earnings, offered to pay half the meal break, and rejected the 40.5–37.5 hours claim.

So the final claim and offer were much closer – though still a good distance apart. There was, too, a considerable degree of common ground. For operatives, the highest-paid grade, both the union and the company were agreed on the weekly basic rate (£93.75), bonus (£35.63), and shift premium (£14.06). The union wanted its 40.5–37.5 hours payments (worth £7.50) and the company offered a shift bonus payment (£5.34). The union's meal-break claim was £9.37, and the company's offer £3.13. So the final figures for the grade were for a union claim of £160.31 a week, with the company offering £151.91 – a difference of £8.40

As provided for under the agreement with the company, EETPU officials then decided to put the issue to binding, pendulum arbitration. Acas was called in, and on 10 January 1986 John Davies, a barrister, was appointed as arbitrator under strict agreed terms of reference: 'The parties ask that the arbitrator finds either for the company's final offer, or for the trade union's final claim in connection with the implementation of a double day-shift system.' At a hearing at Acas' head office the following month, each side argued its case, and on 12 March, Davies delivered his historic judgement – the first ever pendulum arbitration award in a strike-free deal.

Davies made clear his unhappiness: 'I have not found this an easy reference to decide and in a sense the pendulum nature of the arbitration has added to my difficulties, because the usual arbitrator's refuge of compromise is not available to me.'[12] He praised the company's approach: 'This is certainly not a case of a stubborn management refusing to recognise the inevitable, for indeed they have shown themselves to be forward-looking and clearly pride themselves upon the good working relationships which they have been able to establish.' But, in the end, he was – as he had to be – unequivocal: 'I find myself more cogently persuaded by the union's argument as to the economic realities of the market place' – in particular, with the information on comparable rates and the impact on employees' working lives of the change to a shift system. Declaring the union's argument to be the 'stronger case', Davies hoped that once shift working got underway at the plant the company's 'cash flows will rapidly relieve any discomfort which this award may cause them.'

Bowman Webber was reluctant, but accepted it; the EETPU was jubilant, and proclaimed it. For the union, Bill Gannon, the executive council member for the area, said it proved the system worked in practice, and that the union had avoided making a claim which the arbitrator would find unreasonable. Roy Sanderson said: 'This is an absolute justification of pendulum arbitration. It proves it is the best dispute-solving mechanism available in industrial relations.' For the company, Thomas Bailey, its finance director, said he hoped the award would help damp down the plant's inter-union difficulties – a covert reference to the strike of a few months earlier.

FTAT claims that the strike which hit the company in January (the EETPU and the company say it was unofficial; FTAT says that the EETPU gave it official sanction) was over the imposition of double day-shift working. The company says the strike, which lasted for about ten days and which involved almost fifty of the plant's 125 employees, was over dismissal action against three employees, one of whom had been voted in as an EETPU shop steward the night before he was warned of his dismissal. Aside from the details of the strike itself, what the Bowman Webber stoppage showed was evidence for the claims of both the supporters and detractors of strike-free deals. Opponents of the deals claim that they do not work, that they cannot provide outbreaks of fireflash industrial action, often unofficial; the strike supports that. But they also claim that the deals take away the employees' right to strike; Bowman Webber's experience rebuts that. Some hard-line proponents of the deals see them as the way to end strikes; clearly, Bowman Webber shows that that is not the case, and that, as the EETPU has claimed for them, all they can do is make strikes less likely; they cannot ultimately prevent them. At Bowman Webber, pendulum arbitration won the plant's employees more money than they could otherwise have got, certainly without striking and maybe even – perhaps especially even – if they had taken action. But the outbreak of a strike shows again that the longer-term impact of the new strike-free deals is still far from clear.

9

Strike Free: New Ways in Old Industries

Strike-free deals, on the experience of Hitachi, Sanyo and Bowman Webber, are clearly far from free of problems. But their advocates argue strongly that they are a good deal freer of difficulty than the industrial relations practices they are replacing. Though the take-up of such a new idea remains small, other employers, and other unions, have begun to note closely the developments being forged by the EETPU.

In addition to the EETPU's range of deals, principally though not solely in electronics companies, NEK Cables, the Norwegian computer and telecommunications cable manufacturer, reached in early 1982 with the GMBATU a single-union, strike-free deal for its Washington plant on Tyneside. Townsend Thoresen in 1984 entered an unusual form of strike-free arrangement for ships operating from its continental ferry port in Portsmouth, under which Channel Stevedores, a loading company, guaranteed uninterrupted freight handling. The company said in its agreement with Townsend Thoresen that it would 'provide for continuity of working free from industrial disruption over the period of the agreement. In the event of this condition not being fulfilled, Thoresen Car Ferries would have the right to consider the agreement to have been breached.' Breach of the agreement would allow Townsend to sue for breach of contract, under normal commercial law. Townsend Thoresen reached a further deal, providing for binding arbitration, which both the company and the union involved thought would facilitate the resolution of disputes without recourse to industrial action, for its ferry services from Dover, following a difficult dispute in late 1985 and early 1986 which halted all services for three weeks. Silentnight, the Lancashire bed manufacturer, reached a two-year strike-free and

pay deal in 1985 with a new workforce, following the dismissal of its original labour force in a strike over pay. Eatons, the US vehicle-component manufacturer signed in January 1986 a single-union, strike-free deal with the AUEW for its Newton Aycliffe plant in Co. Durham.

But perhaps the most significant dispersal of strike-free arrangements came when the agreements were taken into wholly new territory – in each case, areas with very traditional industrial relations practices: motor manufacture and newspaper publishing.

Motor Manufacture

'Imagine,' runs the voice, soft and comforting, but optimistic – futuristic, too:

> Imagine a car factory where no one goes on strike, and where no one is made redundant either. Imagine if the managing director dressed just the same as the men on the line. Imagine if the management and the workers got together every day to see how they could make things better. Imagine if work wasn't just about getting a better pay packet, but about working together to make something you could be proud of. Maybe then it would be possible to make a car so good, they'd have a 100,000 mile, or three-year warranty. Or is this just a day dream?

The voice and synthesiser music stops, a blue-jacketed figure rubs away the dreamy view, and the word stands revealed: NISSAN. The punchline is neat, punning, memorable: 'Nissan. They don't half work.'

Nissan's television advertisements – designed by Saatchi and Saatchi, the Conservative Party's image-makers – stressed in their first words the new company's strike-free status. The deal signed by Nissan in April 1985 drew widespread attention, far more than any of the other strike-free agreements which it closely resembles. An Industrial Society conference on the deal drew for its audience a virtual who's who of British companies: Amoco, the Bank of England, British Rail, British Steel, Esso, Ferranti, ICI, National Bus, Pilkington, Perkins Engines, Reed International, Rolls Royce, TI – and included two companies, Silentnight and Times Newspapers, which six months later had both put strike-free deals to their workforces.

Nissan's personnel director, Peter Wickens, a forceful, fluid and articulate advocate of the agreement and especially of the philosophy underlying it, acknowledges that it is largely not new: 'My contribution is to distil from my background of American, British, German and Japanese management what is best for us.' But the agreement *is* significant, on three principal counts: it took the idea and the practice of strike-free deals into a wholly new industrial area, motor manufacturing – and one which perhaps better than many exemplifies traditional UK industrial relations; it brought into the field a major union, the engineering workers; and unlike many of the other strike-free deals, it was not born out of crisis, but stemmed from careful consideration and planning, from a clear sense of objectives to be achieved.

Nissan needs to avoid strikes. Competition has increased the importance to motor manufacturers of not losing production time, not losing sales, through strikes. But Nissan was entering an industry which has one of the highest strike records in the UK: in 1983, the motor industry's strike rate was almost ten times higher than the average.[1] Accordingly, Nissan needed to plan, and plan carefully, to try to avoid them. The care in the company's preparation was evident too in its painstaking search to find a site for its UK base – one of the most exhaustive location searches in commercial history, looking at more than fifty sites in all, with local authorities vigorously bidding against each other for the development. Nissan ended up eventually on 800 acres of a former municipal airport near Washington, in the job-hungry north-east ('We need a Nissan once a week,' said a Sunderland workshop manager).[2]

Bidding was also fierce in industrial relations terms: Acas, for example, arranged for the company a series of meetings with managers and trade unionists in Cardiff, Leeds, London and Newcastle as part of Nissan's familiarisation with UK practices – and as part of the UK unions' pitch. Pitch they did, hard, too – and all of them: the TGWU, the AUEW, the GMBATU. Britain's major unions lined themselves up for inspection by the Japanese in a way never seen previously: 'We were forced to parade before prospective employers like beauty queens,' says Joe Mills, the TGWU's northern regional secretary. Embarrassing, irritating, but there were to be new jobs – up to 2700 by the end of the planned second phase of the development, making cars in the UK from scratch, rather than assembling them, kit-form – and new union members were the prize. Reluctant or not, it is a contest most unions would go through again if they felt they had to. 'I suspect we would all be on parade again,' says Tom Burlison, northern regional secretary of GMBATU.

Nissan thought hard about a non-union operation: 'We considered the alternatives of no trade unions, and a multiplicity of trade unions,' Wickens says. 'We rejected the first because it would lead to several years of counter-productive antagonism, and the latter because sooner or later it would lead to an erosion of our flexibility and single-status objectives.'[3] Wickens believes single unionism is vital: 'However strongly two or more unions might have agreed to work together in a more co-operative environment, problems would sooner or later arise which would start to bring in traditional British demarcations.'[4] Wickens says that all the unions involved – including the TGWU, one of the most vociferous critics of the strike-free deals – offered the company similar arrangements, but it eventually settled on the AUEW because it felt that this was the union to which most employees in the north-east would feel easiest in belonging.

Competition over, the other unions in effect withdrew, leaving Nissan to negotiate the new deal, unofficially assisted by Acas, with the engineering workers' local divisional organiser, Joe Cellini, twenty years a full-time AUEW official, and George Arnold, his predecessor in the job – elected from it to the union's national executive. The agreement which Cellini, Arnold and Wickens reached blended their experience, drew from developing current practice – all pay agreements under it, for instance, will normally last for two years, rather than the traditional twelve months – and learnt from the strike-free deals which had gone before it. The method of disputes resolution was especially sophisticated. Committed firmly to resolving disputes in-house, if necessary the two sides would go outside to conciliation by Acas – an important insertion, not featured in many of the other strike-free deals, providing a useful degree of flexibility. Then, as the agreement states, 'in the event of conciliation not producing a solution both parties may agree to arbitration.' Arbitration would be pendulum, and binding. The key word is 'may'. Though the deal stipulates that 'during the course of such negotiations, conciliation or arbitration there will be no industrial action' – a straightforward (for these deals) no-strike clause – the conditional, non-mandatory arbitration clause allows both the company and the union to insist that it is not a no-strike deal, but one designed to avoid strikes. Theoretically, at least, it would be possible for a strike to occur after Acas conciliation, if there was no agreement to proceed to arbitration. Possible, but unlikely, according to those workers already taken on. Ed Handyside, a supervisor, describes strike action at Nissan as 'very unlikely'. George Stangrew, a team leader, says: 'I can't envisage any issue which is likely to cause a strike but which can't be resolved by other means.'[5]

But Stangrew points out, too, a further crucial element of the Nissan package. In relation to his own point about strikes, he says: 'Most of the people we are employing here at the minute are all of that attitude.' Selection of staff was painstaking. With high unemployment – 20 per cent in the surrounding area at the beginning of 1986 – the company had a huge labour pool in which to fish: 3500 applied for its first twenty-two appointments, as supervisors. Nissan could winnow out those applicants who possessed the qualities it wanted – a positive, constructive attitude towards the company, reducing the risk of conflict from selection onwards. Of the twenty-two supervisors, for instance, only six had previous experience of working in the motor industry; that mix, or a lower proportion, has been followed in the workforce more generally. All twenty-two supervisors were flown to Japan for two months to learn about the company and the way it works. Steve Milner, formerly a frozen-food factory foreman, said: 'One big difference you immediately notice in Japan is that they respect people who make things. In Britain people look down on you if you work in a factory.' Colin Graham, who used to work at Ford, said: 'I wouldn't like to run down the Ford Motor Company, but what I find refreshing is the degree of teamwork that exists at Nissan.'[6]

Nissan's employees may not be making such comparisons in public – but Nissan's advent in the UK car market (substantially increasing its share of it, too, well before production even began at Washington) forced the other motor manufacturers to make them themselves. Liking what they saw proved to be impossible. According to figures supplied by the companies, their cumulative losses over the ten years to 1983 were: Vauxhall – 1.2 million days lost through strikes (125,100 cars lost); Ford – 4.9 million days (563,200 cars); and BL – 15.8 million days (756,200 cars).[7] Faced both with a strike-free Nissan planning in its second phase to build 100,000 cars a year in the north-east, and with their own appalling strike records, the other companies had to act. They did.

BL launched a wholesale change in its previously highly abrasive management style, using a consultants' company to draw upon a wide range of management practices – including those of the

Japanese – in an effort to seek employee co-operation and commitment to the company's prosperity.[8] Its moves included Nissan-style recruitment selection; the introduction of zonal, or quality, circles; and greatly improved communication, including track-by-track television screens for immediate company information. Ford in its 1985 pay negotiations put forward proposals for extensive job flexibility, operators' own cleaning of work areas, and the amalgamation of job titles into one single lineworker job. Vauxhall, in a move eventually approved at local level, sought a new reinforcement to its traditional *status quo* disputes procedure. The document which it put to its unions in summer 1985 made clear what the cause of its action was:

> If other companies with their trade unions can come up with so-called 'no-strike' agreements, which basically means no action until the procedure is exhausted, we have the right to insist that all employees observe [the *status quo*] clause of the existing procedure, and thus we would enjoy the same benefits as trade unions are giving employers elsewhere.

Ken Gill, 1985–6 TUC chairman, sees a different connection: 'The fact is there is a finite level of motor-car sales in Britain, and what Nissan gets, BL loses. Jobs will be destroyed.' He feels that 'if Nissan succeeds in reaching the level of production it forecasts the devastation of the Midlands motor-car industry will accelerate.'[9] Gill objects to Nissan's strike-free deal. But from his point of view, at least it could have been worse. Would Nissan have liked a wholly no-strike deal? 'Yes, probably we would have liked it,' says Peter Wickens, 'but I'm also a realist. What I would very much prefer is an agreement that can be made to stick, rather than an agreement which goes to the ultimate, but which you can't necessarily make stick.'

Newspaper Production

Aristocrats of labour: for long, printers on Britain's national newspapers enjoyed the rank, wealth and privileges accorded to their unofficial status in the UK labour movement. Possibly alone among groups of employees, Fleet Street printers seemed immured from the effects of the recession which swept through other groups of workers and their unions, scaling down their visions of what was possible, forcing them to keep their heads down. Not so the Fleet

Street members of the NGA craft and Sogat '82 general print unions, who took to extremes the basic model of trade unionism: obtaining the best possible terms and conditions for the union's members. In a sense, they were the ultimate Thatcherite unions. 'There's a kind of Conservatism about them,' says Tom Rice, the EETPU's national newspaper officer. 'They're into monopoly capitalism.'[10] These unions were working solely within the peculiar market forces which operated in the national newspaper industry; the combination of high potential profit, cut-throat competition, and a uniquely perishable product made newspaper managements keen, sometimes desperate, to produce their papers, at whatever the immediate cost. 'How do you deal with the unions?' Sir Keith Joseph, then education secretary, asked Mirror Group managers (pre-Robert Maxwell ownership) at a lunch. 'By giving in,' came the honest answer. 'Incomes of £30,000–40,000 a year are commonplace among Fleet Street printers,' Lord Marsh, chairman of the Newspaper Publishers' Association, said at the start of 1986. 'Holidays of eight, ten, twelve weeks are commonplace. A working week of twenty-four hours is commonplace.'

Why then, amidst all this power, all this privilege, all this deft manipulation of market forces, did the same print unions come, in January 1986, to be putting these proposals to a national newspaper management:

Binding arbitration – and a strike-free clause. 'We are prepared to agree a procedure which provides for the discussion of company-related affairs, and the resolution of problems, and, as such, precludes the necessity for recourse to any form of industrial action by the company, the union or the employees. This would include provision in its final stages for conciliation by Acas, and ultimately, binding arbitration which could be triggered unilaterally by one party.'

Flexibility. 'Technology and working methods being used would necessitate flexible working and affect traditional areas of jurisdiction. In the event of agreement between the unions not being possible, there would be adjudication by the TUC with a binding award.'

Advisory board. 'We would wish to see established an advisory board comprising representatives of the company and unions to review the performance and plans of the company and to provide consultation and discussion on all aspects of the company's operations.'

Single status. 'We believe that the company should provide single status for all employees with common conditions of employment.'

Bargaining unit. Though there would be more than one union, it is the unions' aims 'to combine as many elements of the employment relationship as possible into a joint comprehensive agreement'.

Overall, the unions stated: 'We do accept that it is in the shared interests of the company, its employees and the unions that we all have a common commitment to profitability, efficiency, harmonious relations, productivity and flexibility, and job security.'

These draft proposals are significant for three reasons: first, that they existed at all; secondly, that they are almost exactly modelled on the strike-free agreements signed by the EETPU and other unions which Fleet Street print union members had been foremost in abusing; and thirdly, *that they were rejected by the company*. Stunned, the print unions could hardly believe it. Brenda Dean, Sogat '82 general secretary, described the proposals as 'really radical'; her opposite number at the NGA, Tony Dubbins, called them 'the best ever offered by any union to any national newspaper employer'.

How could the mighty be so humbled? How, in the words of one analysis at the time, is it that 'the powerful print unions, the NGA and Sogat '82, are agreeing to deals they would have lit their branch secretaries' cigars with only a year ago'?[11] Principally, the reason was that just as Fleet Street's print workers seemed economically cocooned, so did its newspapers: burdened with overweening labour costs certainly, but, for that very reason, safe – a cartel, a magic circle into which no outsider could break, leaving its own economics crazy but insulated. The print unions and the newspapers knew that at some point it would all change; but not just yet, dear Lord, not just yet.

But the economics of the industry did change. In the provinces, free newspapers, initially badly produced and carrying little more than advertising, began to appear. Dismissed at first, they prospered, grew better, challenged, combated and then started seeing off their paid-for rivals. Using low-cost production, rooted in computer-based technology and contract printing, they presented more normal provincial papers with a stark choice: change or go under. To survive, they would have to cut back their own cost bases; that meant bringing in the more efficient new technology, widely used in non-UK newspapers – and that meant in turn a fight with the print unions, principally the NGA. From the Nottingham *Evening Post* onwards, where the NGA was simply ejected by the management, the rearguard action commenced.

Crucial to it was the 1983 dispute between the union and Messenger newspapers, based in Stockport and Warrington, whose proprietor was a hustling entrepreneur called Eddie Shah.[12] It was a dispute which was significant in a whole range of ways, from the first 'success' of the TUC's new realism, to the first achievement of a new style of policing industrial disputes. The Warrington dispute carried with it two crucial lessons for the newspaper industry: it showed that the NGA could be beaten, and it showed *how*. The last point was vital. One effect of the decline of union power in the recession was that the Government's labour legislation on picketing and on secondary industrial action had barely been used, because few unions had any longer the strength to mount something vigorous enough to warrant it. The NGA had; but Shah hit back, hauling the union into court, forcing the seizure of its assets and eventually causing it the loss of a total of £2 million in fines and other costs. The NGA retired hurt, while Shah bided his time, until Andrew Neil, editor of the *Sunday Times*, who had become close to Shah during the dispute, and whose technological bent was becoming increasingly frustrated by resistant national newspaper print practices, first proposed the idea to Shah of setting up a new national daily paper.

Like many breakthroughs, it was essentially simple – transferring the new operational methods of the provinces to the national stage. Shah brought in a complete computer-based typesetting system for his new paper, *Today*, hired a small number of journalists – and then reached agreement on a single-union, strike-free deal for all the non-journalistic staff with the EETPU. The formal ranks of the UK labour movement were agape, their wildest nightmare come true: how *could* even the EETPU, pariahs extraordinaire, lie down with Shah after the Warrington dispute? But they could, and did; they even tried to mediate – for a day – to bring the other print unions into the building. The EETPU approached Shah. Then, like many of the deals it was now negotiating, the union reached outline agreement with him, the blanks to be filled in later, but the heads of agreement contained the full set of provisions of the strike-free package: single unionism, flexibility, single status, company advisory board, pendulum arbitration, no strikes. There were some other provisions: a share option scheme, for instance, which Shah strongly favoured.

The strike-free deal with the electricians was the key element in

Shah's radical mix. The TUC's proposed newspaper of a few years previously, for instance, foundered on the rock of the issue of labour costs, which its feasibility study carefully tried to avoid considering in depth. But with the hands of the NGA's members off the keyboards, slashing costs was possible. At the Kent *Messenger*, for example, when NGA members there went into dispute in April 1985, the company paid young, female secretaries to input copy at a fraction of the NGA cost. Shah bought his own presses, so his start-up costs of £13 million were higher than they would otherwise have been. But stripping out that cost, the implication was astonishing: instead of costing anything up to £300 million to start up a new paper, it could now be done for as little as £5 million.

The floodgates opened: at one point, it seemed that new national newspapers were being announced on a weekly basis, with five promised by the end of 1985. Established, traditional Fleet Street – the companies, not the unions – could, perhaps, try to ignore one Shah as a gadfly, no threat: a whole host was impossible. Lumberingly, the established papers began to move: the Telegraph and Express groups announced job cuts. Robert Maxwell repeatedly cried 'change – or closure', eventually securing 2100 redundancies which, he claimed, would enable a new lean and efficient *Mirror* to take on the new competition. As well as his massive attitudinal shift, Shah moved physically, too, away from Fleet Street, to Pimlico. The other papers dusted off their plans to quit their traditional home, too, heading east for London's derelict docklands, where land was relatively cheap, and available: new sites, new practices, new opportunities.

Foremost among them was Rupert Murdoch's News International. His long-idle £100 million plant just east of Tower Bridge, at Wapping, had grown to seem like a white elephant, never to be used because of the inability of unions and management to reach agreement on it. Shah changed all that: from a white elephant, Murdoch transformed Wapping into a technological fortress, all shining computers inside, all rolls of barbed wire out. The proposal was to print from there a new London evening paper, the *Post*; the print unions suspected a feint, masking the real intention of shifting the printing to Wapping of the Murdoch titles, *The Times* and *Sunday Times*, and the *Sun* and *News of the World*. To cover the Wapping operation, Murdoch put to the unions a set of proposals, to which they were highly unlikely ever to agree. The proposals were astonishing, for anywhere in British industry, let alone for national newspapers. They were for a legally binding deal, which would allow the company to sue the unions unlimitedly if the contract was broken by industrial action; and a fearsome no-strike clause – neither the union nor its members would 'instigate, promote, sponsor, engage in, finance or condone any strike or other industrial action for any reason whatever . . . all employees who take part in strike or other industrial action will be subject to immediate dismissal, and shall have no right to appeal against dismissal under the disciplinary procedure.' Other proposals included: no closed shop; unprecedented management rights to manage; binding arbitration; complete labour flexibility; and – not unusual anywhere else, but staggering for Fleet Street, where the print union chapels had long controlled the supply of labour – manning levels to be determined by the employer.

The print unions were not opposed to moving to Wapping – physical conditions at the *Sun*'s Bouverie Street site, for instance, were poor; nor were they opposed to new technology *per se*, as could be seen in a report by Brenda Dean, who had led a team to study newspapers in north America: 'Opposing technological change is not an option for trade unions in printing – it is simply a rapid road to de-unionisation.'[13] They tried hard. For years, the NGA had seen direct entry – journalists and advertisement copytakers typing material directly into production computers, rather than having it retyped by NGA members – as the ultimate sacrifice. But they conceded it for the *Post* – and were then thunderstruck when the company dismissed it as *insufficient*.

As with Shah, the role of the EETPU was crucial. Following the Shah deal, the electricians had chanced their arm when they could, tossing in an offer to Maxwell of a single-union, strike-free deal for the Mirror group. But at Wapping, they had a dual track: unprecedentedly, they indicated that they had no objections in principle to signing a legally binding deal (though the real game plan was to get into a position to negotiate Murdoch down to a more normal strike-free agreement). That strengthened Murdoch's hand in his talks with the print unions, for the electricians provided a fallback for the company, effectively an alternative labour force with which it could commission the plant, and in time – when the inevitable dispute erupted with the two main print unions – print the papers, producing in January 1986 the UK's first-ever non-union national newspapers.

In desperation, and fronted by Norman Willis, the TUC general secretary, the print unions at Brenda Dean's instigation tried to capture the electricians' ground as the electricians had seized their jobs, by offering to Murdoch an EETPU-style strike-free package; to no avail.

At the same time, the TUC arraigned the EETPU before the full court of the General Council, and charged it with improper activities over Wapping. Hammond hit back with a lengthy document rebutting the accusations, claiming that the union didn't know about the recruitment of its members to run the Wapping plant; but it was no good – they didn't believe him. Instead, the EETPU was placed under a series of directives about its conduct over the dispute. From that moment, the strained relations between the TUC and the EETPU markedly began to improve, and the electricians started to play a key role in paving the way for further talks between the company and the print unions. It was a long, hard grind, marred outside the plant itself by violence on a scale not seen since the miners' strike; it led eventually to a final offer from Murdoch, made at a Heathrow hotel, of the company's old *Sunday Times* printing plant and £50 million in compensation money for those sacked when Murdoch staged his *coup d'état*.

Against the background of the deskilling of traditional printers by the use of computers, and the wholesale alteration of the industry's economics signalled by Shah (however poor his paper, *Today*, actually was when it first appeared), Wapping fundamentally changed the balance of power in Fleet Street – long tipped, heavily, in favour of the unions – towards management. For the traditional print unions, pushing back the pendulum may prove to be impossible.

10

The Alternative: No Unions, No Strikes

Driving west along the M27 motorway towards Southampton, the plant appears as a monument to modernity: white, mid-1970s at one end, blind windows; then at the opposite end, stark black, an early 1980s addition, with staff visible inside, scurrying, glimpsed through the opaque windows. Standing on land reclaimed from the sea, flanked by ornamental lakes, this is North Harbour, just above Portsmouth. It is the UK headquarters of the world's largest computer company, IBM. Inside, the theme of ultra-modernism is continued – lots of green plants, light tiles, a sense of purposefulness, of confidence. Access for all staff to different parts of the building is by plastic security card; inserted into a wall-mounted reader, it opens the door. The staff restaurant is single-status, and everyone eats there. Overlooking one of the decorative pools, it serves – very efficiently – four main courses each day. It is all reminiscent of the new, high-tech Habitat. Sleek, groomed, North Harbour has the feel of success – and no wonder.

IBM bestrides the computer industry like a colossus. 'No one ever got fired for buying an IBM' is an industry truism – and one which has seen off many of its competitors. In every sector of the industry in which it operates – mainframes, storage devices, personal computers, electronic typewriters – it dominates, clustering parasitic companies around it, and allowing others to plug the few holes it has left. In the first three quarters of 1985, the company reported lower earnings than previously, reflecting the limited fallback in the US high-tech industries, though its fourth quarter results improved markedly, with a 23.4 per cent rise in net income – evidence of a cautious but sustained upturn in high-tech. 'The industry went through a tough time in 1985,' said Tony Cleaver, chief executive of

IBM (UK), at the beginning of 1986. 'It has come out of that period with a better understanding of what has to be done to ensure growth in the future.'[1]

In the UK, IBM now employs more than 18,000 people in about forty locations – manufacturing, sales, and service sites. Multinational, the company is acutely aware of international differences, as Kap Cassani, chairman IBM Europe/Middle East/Africa, told an OECD conference in Paris in November 1985: 'In Europe in certain circles there is still an antagonism to business, particularly small business, as a respectable pursuit for able minds. No such stigma exists across the Atlantic. . . . Europe's greater social stability may be enviable, but today's unemployment may be too high a price for it, and that stability is itself now threatened.'[2] Nevertheless, the company's commitment to the UK is considerable. Manufacture for the whole of Europe of its highly successful personal computer, for instance, is carried out at its Greenock plant, in Scotland's Silicon Glen – its first factory in the UK, established in 1951. Its development laboratory at Hursley, near Winchester, is one of the company's largest outside the USA. IBM (UK) is successful, too: its profits for 1985 were up by 60 per cent, to £308 million, in a year when the company world-wide was struggling. Its turnover rose by 30 per cent to £3.04 billion, considerably higher than any of IBM's other European operations. Cleaver says: 'I believe that, today, IBM has a greater growth potential in the UK than in almost any other country.'[3]

IBM: Employees

Growth the company has already seen – in revenue, in exports, in profits. It has seen, too, a remarkable growth in employment (see Figure 10.1). In 1984, its recruitment of 1744 new employees was nearly double the 1983 figure, and the highest for ten years; the 363 new graduates taken on was the highest number ever in one year. Employment has risen less sharply than it did during the extraordinary acceleration in the heady days of the late 1960s, though its growth is startling at a time when employment generally is falling. Of its workforce, by far the largest proportion (almost 95 per cent) are full-time, permanent employees; another 3 per cent or so are on assignment overseas, with just over 1 per cent on secondment, maternity leave, or otherwise deemed to be inactive, and a little more than that part-time. Senior managers have little time for theories, even practices, of core and peripheral labour, a complex combination of full-time and temporary workers. The company's age range is higher than some in the electronics industry: the largest single segment of its workforce is in early middle age, with a quarter over the age of forty and 10 per cent over fifty. Its average age was over thirty-seven in 1984. The largest portion (38 per cent) work in marketing and services, with 27 per cent in manufacturing. Pay, for most, is relatively high, with well over half earning more than £10,000 a year by the beginning of 1985. Most employees stay with the company: average labour turnover in IBM has stood for some years at about 2.5 per cent; the concept of an 'IBM-er' (significantly, not an employee who identifies particularly strongly with the company, but simply an employee) is widely voiced in the company's sites. Almost a third of all UK employees have been with IBM for more than fifteen years; the average length of service is eleven and a half years.

IBM: Strikes and Unions

That kind of satisfaction with the company is reflected in other ways too. As a memorandum from the company put it in early 1985: 'The company has never lost a single day's production through disputes.'[4]

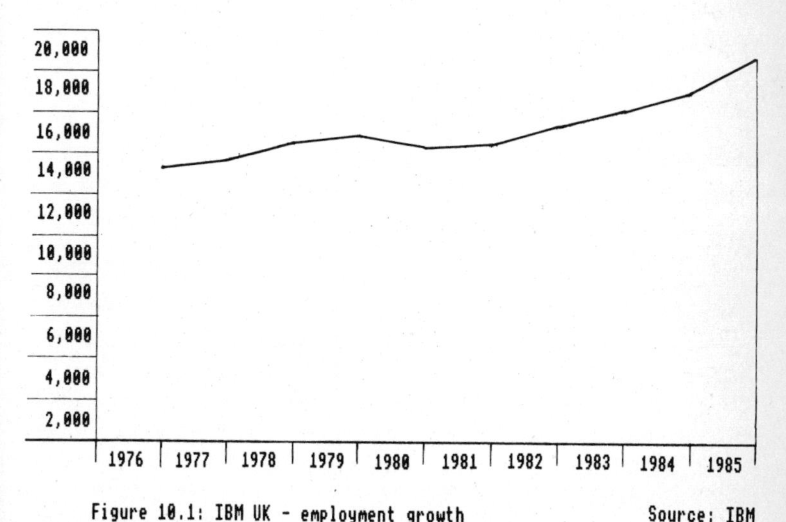

Figure 10.1: IBM UK - employment growth Source: IBM

IBM does not have strikes. 'Since IBM United Kingdom was founded in 1951,' it says, 'there have been no strikes or lay-offs in the company. Much of this success is due to IBM's belief in respect for the individual.'[5] One aspect of that philosophy is that IBM does not recognise trade unions. It is widely seen by union activists as an anti-union company. Even senior officials of the EETPU, the UK union rated most highly, indeed almost solely, by the company's senior managers, charge that IBM in Scotland has persuaded electronics companies there towards non-unionism, establishing a virtual anti-union cartel. But IBM insists that it is not anti-union; publicly, it is neutral, non-union. Its handbook for employees is specific:

> You have the right, if you so desire, to be a member of any trade union you choose and if you are a member of a trade union you have the right at the appropriate times to take part in the activities of the union, to seek appointment or election as an official of that union, and if appointed or elected to hold office. You also have the right, if you so desire, not to be a member of a trade union or other organisation of workers.[6]

What that is *not* specific about is that the company in the UK does not recognise unions for collective bargaining purposes. Implicitly, IBM sees in the concept of unionisation the assumption that the interests of the employed would inevitably be neglected by the employer in the absence of trade union representation. IBM does not accept this, arguing instead that its record shows that it is possible for a company to be successful, to be managed successfully, and for its employees' best interests to be a central part of that. Overall, it maintains that it does not recognise unions because its employees do not want it to.

That has only been tested once – but the results were so conclusive that the UK unions now effectively do not consider IBM as a likely or possible area for recruitment. In 1977, under the statutory recognition provisions then still in force under the Labour Government, the conciliation service Acas was asked by a number of unions – ASTMS, AUEW, Tass and the EETPU – to consider a claim for recognition at the Greenock plant. Each union claimed that it had the most support there – sufficient for recognition to be granted as a way in to greater trade union organisation throughout the company. ASTMS claimed seventy-five members there; the Acas survey found twenty-seven.[7] The EETPU claimed fifty to a hundred; Acas

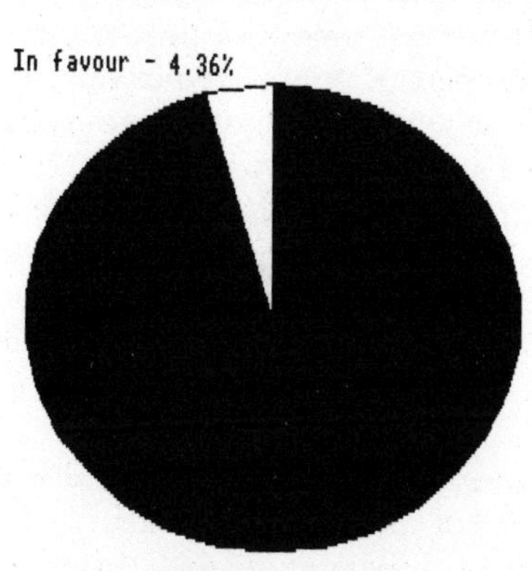

Figure 10.2: IBM employees' support for collective bargaining   Source: Acas

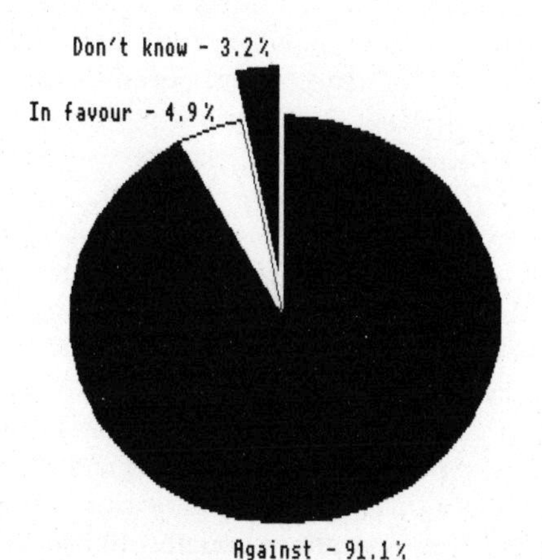

Figure 10.3: IBM UK employees wanting to join a trade union   Source: Acas

found seven. AUEW and Tass between them claimed 500. Acas found nine. The Acas survey showed the level of trade unionism across the whole company. Given that unions are not recognised by IBM, the fact that 99.2 per cent of those responding (a high response rate: 95.2 per cent of all employees) were not in unions is perhaps not that surprising. But at that time, the high-water mark of post-war British trade unionism, throughout the company only 4.9 per cent (8.9 per cent at Greenock) wanted a union to bargain for them with the company; even among trade union members, about a quarter were against collective bargaining. Among non-union members, 91.1 per cent said they would not join a union even if IBM recognised it (see Figures 10.2 and 10.3).

IBM: Employment Practices

It is hardly surprising, then, that IBM should have maintained its policy of not sanctioning unions. That policy runs deep: IBM refuses to recognise unions, not because of their potential nuisance value, but because their collectivism runs wholly counter to the company's fundamentally individualist philosophy. IBM lists three beliefs as the essence of its corporate culture, that indefinable but vitally important element of its make-up which, senior managers testify, allows them to walk into any IBM site, anywhere in the world, and feel at home. The beliefs are respect for the individual, service to the customer, and the pursuit of excellence. Though these credos seem Japanese-like in their moral idealism, the IBM way – though it achieves the high standards of performance and output characteristic of the Japanese, including Japanese companies in the UK – is exactly opposite to the Japanese method. Japanese companies, including those in the UK, forge a corporate whole through collectivism, made most obviously manifest in the rigorous similarity of the uniforms which employees are required to wear. There are no uniforms at IBM; even the coffee served by machines in the North Harbour restaurant is individually ground. With near-boyish enthusiasm, IBM managers proclaim with pride a long-standing, in-house description of the company's employees: 'The biggest boy scout troop in the world.' Precisely; the company and its employees are characterised by exactly that combination of individualist entrepreneurship, within an overall corporate philosophy – and it is, crucially, a proselytising philosophy, too: IBM knows it has a message, a better way of doing things.

'They are happy with the company,' says John Steele, director of personnel, of the company's employees, 'happy with the environment and happy with the jobs that they do.' Why? 'There are reasons for that,' says Steele – and those reasons are IBM's complex and interlocking series of employee-relations procedures which both help the company to perform as efficiently as possible and effectively remove the need for trade unions.

Full Employment

IBM (UK) has never had enforced redundancies. It guarantees its employees a job – for life. That job need not necessarily be the same job – jobs will change as the company does, adapting to changes in the computer industry. This approach achieves two opposite, though not mutually exclusive, ends: it generates a feeling of security, and it instils an acceptance of change as a fact of employment. To meet its ambition, and to meet the changes in the market, the company has to operate detailed and long-range manpower planning systems, trying to adjust its intake to what it feels the market is likely to require (but its position in the industry makes it a dominant part of that market; to some extent, indeed perhaps more than most companies, it can shape market forces, as well as be shaped by them).

Single Status

Not just in its restaurants is IBM single-status; in the main, all employees receive the same basic benefits, have the same conditions. There are two principal exceptions. First, though the company does not usually pay overtime ('Overtime is not encouraged as a way of life in IBM. Employees are advised not to rely on overtime earnings as a supplement to their basic income'[8]), it will pay it to 'non-professional employees' – production workers, secretaries, clerical employees – where necessary, and where agreed. Secondly, company cars: some employees, principally sales staff, need a car for their work; others get one as a perk – because they are doing a certain job at a certain level which would tend in outside industry to feature a car as part of its remuneration package. But the company does not regard these as significant blows to its practice of single status; what it sees as much more important are the opportunities such status offers.

Equal Opportunity

That both leads into and stems from the recognition that any employee can make a contribution. Managers point with pride (and optimism) towards those for whom single status and equality of opportunity has combined, with spectacular success – Tony Cleaver, the chief executive, started as an education instructor, and Jim Miller, director of manufacturing, as a customer engineer. At a more global level, for instance, women make up almost a third of the company's workforce, and comprised in 1984 13.2 per cent of its professional workforce, though only 3.4 per cent of its management positions.

Merit Pay

Pay is a central element in collective bargaining. Pay in IBM is not a collective matter for employees, though salary ranges are determined centrally by the company, based on an annual confidential salary survey conducted by IBM among leading companies held by IBM to be comparable. Wage and economic forecasts are taken into account, and mid-points for the salary ranges are then arrived at by the addition of a certain percentage to bring the company's average above the external average.[9] Each autumn the company carries out this exercise, but it is careful to impress upon its employees that increases are not given annually (though most fall in the eleven-to-thirteen-month period). Pay for all employees, other than sales staff, who work on a commission basis, is determined in this way.

But this exercise gives only overall pay boundaries. Individual line managers recommend increases for specific individuals, based on merit, and measured by performance. IBM runs two job-evaluation systems, one for professional and one for non-professional staff, which measure the value of jobs to the company. Performance of individuals is then assessed against this, with managers usually having the flexibility to pay within plus or minus 5 per cent of the overall pay boundaries. Salary ranges run about 15–20 per cent above and below the IBM average at the top and bottom points of the scale.

Performance assessment is a well-established feature. Managers and individuals in their management unit meet to agree 'reasonable' objectives for individual performance. Sometimes these are difficult to arrive at – objective, quantitative standards are hard to find for clerical or managerial work; and the system does place considerable reliance on employees being able to analyse their own performance and likely objectives. The employee signs the lengthy performance form, with the proviso that if the objectives, or the job, change during the performance period, then the criteria will be examined again. In addition, the system has built-in flexibilities: employees who are not performing well will be told by their line manager well before their twelve-month review. At the review stage, employees are scored against their own objectives on a five-point basis. As well as providing the yardstick for pay movements, the system looks at performance more generally: those whose performance is rated at five (not acceptable) could eventually find themselves effectively sacked by the company (in fact, the employee in almost all cases leaves rather than is fired). But such cases are very few – less than 1 per cent of its already low labour turnover figure.

Open Communications

The centre of the company's communications system is the manager–employee relationship. In addition to their occupational responsibilities for the work their section is doing, managers have in effect personnel responsibilities for the staff who work for them (that helps reduce the number of personnel specialists: 285 in all at the beginning of 1986). The ratio is kept deliberately tight: classically in IBM it is one to nine – one manager dealing with nine employees, though it varies according to work area; one to six in marketing, where employees are more mobile, and performance requirements greater, one to fourteen in customer engineering, one to seventeen in manufacturing. All managers receive forty days' training per year – thirty-two of them on people management. 'At the end of the day,' says Steele, 'it's the line manager who is responsible for his or her people – being his or her personnel manager.' This is the key relationship, for appraising performance, career prospects, concerns, though it is backed up with a range of other techniques – company newspapers, financial updates, noticeboards, management information letters, departmental meetings. Employees are also encouraged to consult their second-line manager – their manager's manager – which acts as a check on the system, and on individuals operating it.

In addition, the company mounts every two years an extensive internal opinion survey, which draws very high response rates – 99 per cent among non-managers, 96 per cent among managers. Each survey has about 100 questions, covering the employees' evaluation of the company, their satisfaction with their jobs, their rating of their manager, their views of their duties and responsibilities, and the results provide the company with a constant measurement of change in employee attitudes (over twenty years, if necessary), and of the *company's* own performance: two-way information.

Grievances in IBM

What happens when this extensive system goes wrong? What happens when these personnel practices start producing dissatisfaction? If part of the function of a union at plant level is to negotiate pay and conditions, then another part is often to help employees over the hurdles of their employers' grievance systems. In IBM, the emphasis is on managers resolving any problems. Sometimes, though, managers cannot or will not do so; sometimes, managers are part or all of the problem themselves. So the company has in place, throughout all its operations worldwide, two separate systems of complaint and appeal.

The first, called 'Speak Up!', provides for employees to raise, in confidence, business-related problems. IBM (UK) currently receives about 1000 a year, with three subjects in 1984 amounting to a third of all issues raised – office administration and procedure (16.6 per cent of the total), working environment (10 per cent) and cafeteria and vending machines (6.7 per cent). Virtually none are unsigned – though anonymity is permitted. They are dealt with by a Speak Up! co-ordinator, who will determine the answer to the query and send a written reply. If the points raised suggest a general difficulty, senior managers will ask for indications of their general source, for example a particular section of manufacturing, and deal with the specific problem. Speak Up! letters towards the end of 1985 covered a range of issues, such as alleged discrimination against software ideas in the company's suggestions scheme – a scheme which saved the company some £496,000 in 1984; computer printer noise levels; the issue only of economy-class travel tickets; the lack of paintings and plants in the basement area of the company's South Bank building in central London.

The second system, Open Door, is more substantial, allowing an employee to appeal against a manager's decision. Most problems are resolved at middle- and senior-management level, after the investigator's interventions. The system is quick, too: the investigator has to speak to the people concerned within ten days of appointment, and to tell the appellant if the decision will take longer than two weeks to reach – and why. Appeals may go to any level in the company. 'If in doubt: aim high,' says Hugh ApSimon, former personnel policies manager with IBM (and with some experience of the system – twice as an appellant, twice as a manager being appealed against, and once as an investigator appointed to examine complaints). 'You can go as high as you like. You should certainly go as high as you need.'[10] In practice, managers appoint an investigator when they receive a complaint, if it is not possible for them to handle it personally, and that investigator is charged with the stature of the relevant manager's office. In 1984, for instance, nineteen Open Door cases were dealt with by the IBM UK chairman's office, divided as follows:

Release/dismissal	3
Employee–manager relations	3
Company policies/practices	3
Advancement/promotion	2
Reassignments	1
Pay/compensation	1
Others	6

In these particular cases, ten appeals, or just over half, were dismissed, four were upheld (21 per cent), with five still pending when the figures were compiled. For those which are dismissed, the whole procedure can then start again at a higher level – inside or outside the UK.

From the evidence of its opinion surveys, the company acknowledges that some employees neither understand, nor believe in, the system. In particular, they feel that its use may damage their career prospects. IBM counters this by insisting that it is important for the company to know of problems, in order to resolve them. ApSimon says in reply to the point about career prospects: 'The theoretical answer is that the fact you have made an Open Door appeal will be completely disregarded; will be forgotten. That is, I think, impossible in practice. Your manager is human, and will remember.' But set against that is the check by other managers, who have responsibilities that include making sure other managers manage properly. Clearly, though, there is still some reluctance to use the system – but not enough, not nearly enough, to make trade unions a feasible alternative.

IBM: The Alternative

Seen by some as in some ways the ultimate non-union company, IBM is not everything which that term implies: it manages, without trade unions acting as a constant reminder, to conduct a complex and successful employee-relations policy. Union officials argue that there is no scope in the company for real redress against it, if necessary, no opportunity to do anything but toe the company line, right or wrong. Most companies which are non-union do not have these sort of policies in place. Indeed, when the EETPU signed in late 1985 a single-union agreement with Yuasa Battery, a previously non-union company in South Wales, it was precisely because the company, in growing, had found its own systems of communication (and control) inadequate. Just as many companies now buy in outside services like catering or cleaning, Yuasa simply brought in the EETPU to provide exactly those personnel services it needed. IBM is in some ways the exception to the non-union rule, and the apotheosis of it. It was not without significance that the Conservative Government called in Len Peach, John Steele's predecessor as IBM personnel director, to restructure personnel and industrial relations in the National Health Service. Other companies, looking at IBM's industrially harmonious, strike-free, non-union record, have asked how they could emulate it. Peach replied to one: 'You start thirty years ago.'

11

Strike Free: New Industrial Relations and the Future

Will the new unionism last? Will the new pattern of industrial relations come unstitched? Will it all change when the economic climate improves? Will the pendulum swing back again? Imponderables: for all the indications which are there of an industrial, a cultural, shift, there is no definite, indisputable evidence, nothing that cannot be judged to be temporary, open to change, liable to reversal. Managers, trade unions, employees, will find no ready answers, no tailored solutions to the often deeply personal questions which social, industrial and political change engenders: should we try to bring this in, or to change that? Should we respond to this, or just hope it will disappear? Should I take this decision, go that way or the other? And what will happen to me either way? As News International's Wapping dispute and many others have so graphically illustrated, whole ways of life can rest on such choices, can pivot on decisions taken at moments of acute crisis.

Probably, the best guess that can be made is that at least some of the changes are permanent, that some are too fundamental to be reversed. At least in part, that is because the factors which brought them about still apply: it is as difficult to see the reversal of some of the developments which led to these far-reaching industrial relations changes as it is to see a return to full employment. Unemployment, for instance, shows obstinately few signs of declining rapidly: as 1985 drew to a close, each month's figures were hitting records, even within the confines of the now-established seasonal pattern. Many of its causes cannot be reversed: steelworks, once closed, are not recommissioned; coalmines cannot be reopened; ships made in the Far East are not suddenly going to become vastly more expensive, prompting the revitalisation of British shipyards; Japan looks unlikely to stop needing to export ferociously. Such structural shifts are likely to continue to be reflected in the pattern of employment, too: technological advance will not stop, and if it does not, employers (and often employees too) will want to take advantage of it. That will continue to enforce a restructuring of the workforce, with consequent changes in employee attitudes, in management initiatives and responses. A General Election might alter the pattern; but even, say, if Labour were returned, some of the changes brought about since the end of the 1970s are not reversible solely by political will. Sometimes, too, the will is not there because the changes have widespread support: a future Labour Government will not, for instance, repeal the Conservative legislative provisions on ballots before strikes, or on union executive elections (though it might alter some of the required forms), for the simple reason that no political party would be returned to power on such a platform.

Current, indicated, trends seem likely to continue: no significant increase in the size of the industrial workforce, with a continued growth in more flexible ways of working, more temporary employment, more self-employment, more part-time working, more homeworking, more women, fewer men. Skill distinctions will continue to be blurred by technology, which will also maintain the move towards smaller plants, smaller business units, buying in specialist outside services such as catering, cleaning and security, and others such as software development.

Where will all this leave trade unions? To begin with, non-unionism is likely either to increase or at least to maintain its current share of more than half the workforce. There are now fewer reasons than ever before why an employer starting up should want to include trade unions in the operation. The pressure, and the need, for trade unions is strongest in the traditional industries, though even there it can be avoided, if the will is strong enough: Rupert Murdoch's Wapping operation has demonstrated clearly that even in an industrial area which virtually defines traditionalism, it is perfectly possible for a determined employer to shrug his way clear from normal practices, and make a giant leap towards a wholly different way of working. Unions, too, may have to come to terms with a choice, starkly put, especially by foreign companies, between employment and trade unionism. As Gavin Laird, general secretary of the engineering workers, suggests:

> If the trade union movement was faced with the proposition that if you, the union, insist on recognition, we won't invest here in Great Britain at all, we would say, yes please, come and invest here – and over a period of time, we will convince you that you should recognise trade unions.[1]

There is evidence to support Laird's view that such conversions are possible; but there are many more examples – IBM is only the most prominent and successful among them – that this may be wishful thinking. Nevertheless, employers, and employees too, seem more likely to be convinced of the value of trade unions if they deliver benefits, to both sides, through co-operation, rather than through conflict. Co-operation, in practice, away from the conference-hall rhetoric, has always been extensive, though few unions could match (in reality, perhaps few would want to) the EETPU's Eric Hammond, who has his own, dedicated self-planted flowering cherry tree in a garden by the side of the Hitachi plant in South Wales, reserved for special and distinguished visitors. There has always been co-operation, because it has been *necessary*. 'The employer's control of recognition has always been a crucial determinant of union development,' William Brown, professor at Cambridge University's applied economics department, says. 'Co-operation may be the only means of preventing the expansion of non-union employer practices.'[2] It may; but critics of co-operation argue that it is virtually tantamount to non-unionism anyway, or if not, that it will lead directly to it. Roy Sanderson of the EETPU has given considerable thought to the question of whether the strike-free agreements, for instance, in providing the gains they do for employees, have inherent within them a drift, if not a drive, towards non-unionism:

> The only answer I can come up with is this: if British unions can only survive and prosper in a conflict-dominated industry that has continual disagreements between employers and employees, then we have got no future at all – because if that's the only environment in which we can prosper then we will go down the tubes with British industry.

Co-operation is likely to mesh in with the moves towards decentralisation in companies' operations, so that the focus of trade unions becomes local, fixing on workplace colleagues, and, by extension, through the need to stay in employment, on the business – enterprise unionism. That kind of development will reinforce the new unionism, the overt rejection of the idea of the employer as an enemy, the replacement of the class struggle with the struggle for markets. No longer us (the workers) against them (the management), but us (our company) against them (the competition). Trade unions at their formal, highest levels are unlikely to accommodate easily with this market-based trade unionism: fêting its idealists, who keep alive the socialist flame, has always been a prominent feature of UK unions, even if they had no other views about the development of the new unionism – which they have. 'It's not modern, up-tempo, 21st-century trade unionism,' says Rodney Bickerstaffe of Nupe. 'It's quisling betrayal.' That kind of permanent friction, a wholesale difference in perspective, is likely to continue to pose a threat to the coherence the TUC has managed to maintain, however strained it has been at times. The ideological gap may be too great.

But that may only be at that level of UK trade unionism. Down at workplace level, in a whole string of deals, traditional trade unionism is working, and is being made to work better. Is that incompatible with the new unionism? Are the two entirely separate, though parallel, tracks? The agreements made at Nabisco, or at Borg Warner, or at Shell Stanlow, are not vastly different from some of the strike-free deals signed by the EETPU and other unions; for the TUC to disapprove of one type and not the other is, at least in part, inconsistent.

As the apotheosis of the new trade unionism, the EETPU looks unlikely to change its stance. Far from it; it believes it is cutting a path down which others will follow. 'What the EETPU does today, the rest do tomorrow,' Hammond says. That is at the heart of his own wish not to be expelled from the TUC. Why should he wish otherwise? 'What's the point of moving away from an organisation that is starting to agree with us?' It is indeed a measure of the influence of the electricians' union, and of its impact, how far the TUC and many of the unions within its folds have had to move towards the ground mapped out by the EETPU and the AUEW. Whatever others think of it, the EETPU genuinely sees itself as a revitalising force, rejecting 'left' and 'right' distinctions. 'We do not believe that the traditional labels adequately reflect the real nature of the debate,' says executive councillor Wyn Bevan. 'Far more appropriate is a distinction between conservative and radical trade unions – with the EETPU firmly in the latter camp.'

Its most radical innovations have included the strike-free package. They are few in number – a precedent, perhaps, but not yet a trend. But they will not disappear: they are now unlikely to be rooted out from the companies which feature them, and, as they spread to other areas, the pressure may be on employers to secure them. Developments in both motor manufacture and national-newspaper publishing have shown that they can clearly provide a real competitive advantage, which other companies are then forced, in a variety of ways, to try to match. They have, too, a significant public relations value: as Nissan has shown in its emphasis on the strike-free element in its own advertising, it can be of advantage to an employer, in reaching commercial deals, to be able in effect to guarantee continuity of production in industrial relations terms.

That guarantee is available because the experience so far of the strike-free agreements is that they work, in terms of part at least of their own objectives: almost without exception, at the plants covered by them, there have been no strikes, no stoppages, no days lost, no production halted, as a result of industrial action. Certainly, it is clear from the agreements, and from what those covered by them say, that they cannot, in the final instance, prevent strikes. Employees can, and may, break their own contracts by striking. Most industrial action is short-lived and unofficial, and nothing in the strike-free agreements prevents that. Not an omission; merely a practical recognition of what is possible, and of what is acceptable.

Given the sharp decline in strike action generally, it is more than likely that the companies featuring the strike-free deals might well not have experienced any industrial action anyway in the time during which the deals have been in force. That is a powerful factor for employers to bear in mind, and is clearly part of the answer to the question why the strike-free deals have not spread further and faster, if they are all that their advocates, from both sides of industry, reckon. Partly, the answer may lie in a genuine and powerful suspicion among unions and employers of anything new – particularly when the old systems, at a time of recession, are working well enough in the most obvious sense of there being no interruptions to production. Why should employers change, yielding substantial ground on the disclosure of confidential information, on employee involvement, on status – on the host of ways in which managements have traditionally kept their authority? Why should unions change, why should they abandon the strike, their principal form of leverage, simply because the current climate has effectively forced it into abeyance? Hard questions for those sold on the agreements to answer, and in fact they cannot answer them; they can do no more than point to employer resistance, and acknowledge that beyond the ranks of the EETPU and a small number of other unions, few unions would be willing – at least publicly – to enter into such arrangements.

Their opponents have their answers, though: 'We have been asked whether we would go along with these kind of deals,' says Ken Gill of Tass. 'The answer has always been – absolutely not. And if we lose out, then we lose out. They're really some kind of serfdom. Maybe comfortable serfdom, depends on the circumstances, but serfdom nevertheless.' His electronics officer, Larry Brooke, agrees: 'I believe that the EETPU does not represent a way forward for trade unions in this country. It's opportunist. It's dishonest. It's just meant to advantage the EETPU in areas where they can win the membership, and then go on and get recognition.'

The package is clearly not without its deficiencies. Ken Cameron, general secretary of the Fire Brigades Union, pointedly questions whether pendulum arbitration, for instance, can be applied to problems other than pay: how can it deal with jobs? with redundancies? If a decision went against an employer in such circumstances, Cameron suggests, the employer would either simply buck it, or, if he accepted it, would (on his own terms for wanting the redundancies in the first place) go out of business; either way, the employees lose. Its proponents accept that the package is not perfect. Sanderson, for instance, would like to see some form of financial commitment woven into it, a means whereby the employees feel they have a direct financial interest in the company – much along the lines of the Conservative Government's stress on wider employee share ownership as the real industrial democracy, the real step forward in industrial relations.

But unions may be forced to accept the system, as Laird suggests:

> With incoming, inward investment, a greenfield site, the employer has the ball at his feet, particularly in this age of drastic redundancy. And then they say to us, well, we want a single-union agreement. We want arbitration as a final stage. We will try to convince them that we will achieve that objective without pendulum arbitration. But if, in the final analysis, we are faced with the situation where the employer says to us, the only condition in which we will give you a single-union agreement or

> indeed recognition at all is with pendulum arbitration – it's that or nothing. Then we will take the arbitration – much as we might dislike it.[3]

The TUC, which has moved against single-union deals, and which has grave reservations about no-strike agreements, might dislike it too; but, at the same time, it has sanctioned such developments as possibly the only way in which trade unionism might penetrate new growth areas of the economy which would otherwise be resistant to trade unionism.

> The most practicable way to increase union organisation might be to develop relationships with employers, particularly those opening new plants, and to conclude on the best possible terms. Even though the terms might not be entirely satisfactory they would, nevertheless, lead to unionisation among employees and provide a basis for future claims for improved terms and conditions.[4]

Privately, even some senior figures in the EETPU are not wholly convinced of the strike-free package as the way forward for trade unions, though they cannot see a better one. They are aware that the agreements are to some extent a gamble. 'They may fail,' says Roy Sanderson. 'They may fall flat on their face, and in a few years' time the people in these companies may return to the same old bad habits that we have had in Britain for decades. That's a possibility. But even if it happens, the experiment has been worthwhile.'

Notes and References

Chapter 1: 'Unthinkable Pacts'

1. *Works Management*, September 1985.
2. *Marxism Today*, September 1985.

Chapter 2: Strikes: The British Disease

1. *TUC Strategy*, 1984.
2. Sources for strike statistics are Department of Employment Gazettes, various, plus C. Smith, R. Clifton, P. Makeham, S. Creigh and R. Burn, *Strikes in Britain* (London, 1978). The latter deals with the number of well-known deficiencies in the coverage and measurement of strikes, with consequent qualifications for interpretation.
3. *TUC Annual Report, 1978.*
4. 'New Forms of Work Organisation', *IMS Manpower Commentary*, No. 30, Institute of Manpower Studies, 1985.
5. *IDS Focus*, No. 37, October 1985.
6. *EPIC Survey of Industrial Relations and Employee Communications*, Summer 1985.
7. Smith *et al.*, *Strikes in Britain*.
8. *Ibid.*
9. J. Dunning, *Japanese Participation in British Industry: Trojan Horse or Catalyst for Growth?* (London, 1986).

Chapter 3: The New World of Work

1. Department of Employment Gazettes, various.
2. G. Bain, 'The Changing Context of Industrial Relations in Britain', unpublished internal paper, University of Warwick, August 1985.
3. *Ibid.*
4. *Labour Force Trends*, TUC 1986.
5. Paper to NEDC, 21 November 1985.
6. Survey for NEDC, 21 November 1985.
7. *Planning for Full Employment*, Labour Party, October 1985.

8. DE Gazettes, various.
9. NEDC exercise, various papers.
10. DE Gazettes, various.
11. Segal, Quince and partners, *The Cambridge Phenomenon: The Growth of High-Technology Industry in a University Town* (Cambridge, 1985).
12. D. Keeble and T. Kelly, 'New Firms and High-Technology Industry in the United Kingdom: The Case of Computer Electronics', University of Cambridge, 1985.
13. M. Breheny, P. Cheshire and R. Langridge, 'The Anatomy of Job Creation? Industrial Change in Britain's M4 Corridor', *Built Environment*, Vol. 9, No. 1, 1983.
14. *Report of the 1981 Survey of Employers*, Berkshire County Planning Department, 1982.
15. Keeble and Kelly, 'The Anatomy of Job Creation?'
16. A. Champion and A. Green, 'In Search of Britain's Booming Towns: An Index of Local Economic Performance for Britain', Curds, 1985.
17. *Sunday Times*, 5 August 1984.
18. D. Massey and N. Miles, 'Mapping out the Unions', *Marxism Today*, May 1984.
19. *National Manpower Survey of the British Electronics and Allied Industries, Electronics Location File*, November 1984.
20. *Labour Performance of US Plants in Scotland*, Scottish Development Agency, 1985.
21. 'Union World', Granada TV, May 1985.
22. C. Mulhearn, 'Urban Employment Decline and Labour Movement Response: The Impact of New Technology', paper, Polytechnic of the South Bank, 1984.
23. ASTMS recruitment literature, 1984.
24. Tass recruitment literature, 1985.
25. J. Northcott, M. Fogarty and M. Trevor, 'Chips and Jobs: Acceptance of New Technology at Work', *PSI Report No. 648*, 1985.
26. See, for example, C. Jenkins and B. Sherman, *The Collapse of Work* (London, 1979).
27. E. Batstone, S. Gourlay, H. Levie and R. Moore, *Union Structure and Strategy in the Face of Technological Change* (Oxford, 1986).
28. Northcott *et al.*, 'Chips and Jobs'.
29. Batstone *et al.*, *Union Structure and Strategy*.
30. *Wiltshire Gazette*, Business supplement, Autumn 1985.
31. Engineering Council, *1985 Survey of Chartered and Technical Engineers* (October 1985).
32. IDS Top Pay Unit, *Monthly Review of Salaries and Benefits*, No. 54, August 1985.
33. Engineering Council, *1985 Survey*.
34. Scottish Development Agency, *Labour Performance*.
35. 'National Manpower Survey', *Electronics Location File*.
36. *Personnel Management*, May 1983.
37. *Industrial Relations Journal*, Vol. 16, No. 3, Autumn 1985.

38. *Personnel Management*, May 1983.
39. T. Blackwell and J. Seabrook, *A World Still to Win: The Reconstruction of the Post-war Working Class* (London, 1985).
40. Ibid.
41. F. Craig, *Britain Votes 3: British Parliamentary Election Results 1983* (Chichester, 1984).
42. L. Whitty, 'General Election Results 1983: Detailed Analysis of Trade Union Vote', confidential TULV paper based on MORI survey work, 8 July 1983.
43. *Social Trends*, 1985.
44. R. Waller, *The Almanac of British Politics* (London, 1983).
45. *The Times*, 18 October 1985.
46. *Financial Times*, 18 April 1984.
47. Blackwell and Seabrook, *A World Still to Win*.
48. A. Heath, R. Jowell and J. Curtice, *How Britain Votes* (Oxford, 1985).
49. See, for example, M. Franklin, *The Decline of Class Voting in Britain* (Oxford, 1985).
50. Heath, Jowell and Curtice, *How Britain Votes*.
51. 'Weekend World', London Weekend Television, 29 January 1984.
52. R. Jowell and S. Witherspoon, *British Social Attitudes: The 1985 Report* (Aldershot, 1985).
53. MORI, 'Working in Britain', survey for IBM/Shell/*Sunday Times*, January 1986.
54. D. Blanchflower, 'What Effect Do Unions Have on Relative Wages in Great Britain?', University of Warwick, paper given at conference, Queen Mary College, University of London, 1986.

Chapter 4: New Realism in the Unions

1. *TUC Annual Report, 1983.*
2. *Ibid.*
3. *Ibid.*
4. F. Chapple, *Sparks Fly* (London, 1984).
5. *TUC Annual Report, 1983.*
6. *Ibid.*
7. *TUC Strategy*, 1984.
8. J. Lyons, 'Trade Unions: Which Way to Go?', Unit for Comparative Research on Industrial Relations, University of Sussex, Hitachi Lecture, 1983.
9. 'TGWU Comments on TUC Strategy', unpublished TGWU paper, 1984.
10. *Ibid.*
11. 'TUC Strategy – GMBATU Comments', paper submitted to TUC, 1984.
12. Unpublished letter from Rodney Bickerstaffe, Nupe general secretary, to Len Murray, 1984.
13. *New Socialist*, September 1984.
14. 'NUR Comments on TUC Strategy', unpublished NUR paper, 1984.

15. *Personnel Management*, March 1984.
16. Hansard, House of Commons, 25 January 1984.
17. 'Weekend World', London Weekend Television, 29 January 1984.
18. *Financial Times*, 2 February 1984.
19. *TUC Annual Report, 1984.*
20. *Financial Times*, 4 March 1984.
21. Unpublished TUC finance and general purposes committee paper, 6 November 1985.

Chapter 5: New Trade Unionism: The EETPU

1. *The Union for Your Future*, EETPU, 1984.
2. *Training for a Secure Future*, EETPU, 1985.
3. E. Hammond, 'Why I Back No-Strike Agreements', *Sunday Times*, 29 December 1985.
4. EETPU, *Training for a Secure Future.*
5. EETPU, *The Union for Your Future.*
6. Speech to Conservative Trade Unionists' conference, Blackpool, 1 December 1985.
7. Interviewed by author on 'Face the Press', Tyne Tees TV, 24 March 1985.
8. *Guardian*, 29 January 1985.
9. *The Times*, 4 July 1985.
10. *Ibid.*
11. *EETPU Training Bulletin*, No. 2, November 1983.
12. Unsolicited testimonial, *Contact*, Vol. 15, No. 4, October 1985.
13. Same in letters to Rogers.
14. EETPU AR21 return to Certification Office, No. 101T, received 19 June 1985.
15. M. Hall, 'Centralised Power in the EETPU', unpublished paper, University of Sussex, May 1981.
16. F. Chapple, *Sparks Fly* (London, 1984).
17. *TUC Annual Report, 1983.*
18. EETPU, *Training for a Secure Future.*
19. Hall, 'Centralised Power'.
20. *Ibid.*
21. For detailed accounts of the case, including the trial, see C. H. Rolph, *All Those in Favour? The ETU Trial* (London, 1962); and O. Cannon and J. Anderson, *The Road from Wigan Pier: A Biography of Les Cannon* (London, 1973).
22. *End the Ban: Communist Party Members of the EETPU Present Their Case for Equal Rights in Their Union*, 1980.
23. *Ibid.*, No. 35.
24. *Ibid.*, No. 38.
25. See, for instance, P. Wintour, 'How Frank Chapple Stays on Top', *New Statesman*, 25 July 1980; *Guardian*, 27 August 1980; and Chapple's reply, *Guardian*, 9 September 1980.
26. *Militant*, No. 776, 29 November 1985.

27. Hall, 'Centralised Power'.
28. *Sunday Telegraph*, 15 February 1981.
29. *The Times*, 17 June 1983.
30. *The Political Fund – EETPU Ballot 1985*, EETPU, 1985.
31. *TUC Annual Report*, 1979 to 1984.
32. *Guardian*, 3 December 1985.
33. Speech to IPM conference, Harrogate, 17 October 1985.
34. *Marxism Today*, September 1985.
35. *Focus*, 29 August 1985.
36. 'File on Four', BBC, 27 January 1986.
37. *BLOC Bulletin*, October 1985.
38. EETPU Executive Council minutes, 10 December 1984 and 15 January 1985.
39. J. Gennard, 'The Financial Costs and Returns of Strikes', *British Journal of Industrial Relations*, Vol. XX, No. 2, July 1982.
40. C. Dow, 'Inflationary Pressures and Union Bargaining Power: The Case for Greater Legal Restriction', paper to Public Policy Centre conference, 12 November 1985.

Chapter 6: Strike-Free Agreements: The Package

1. Speech to EETPU biennial conference, Blackpool, 5 July 1985.
2. Acas briefing note to staff, 3/1984.
3. Speech to IPM conference, Harrogate, 18 October 1985.
4. *Personnel Management*, August 1985.
5. *Marxism Today*, November 1984.
6. K. Morgan and A. Sayer, 'A "Modern" Industry in a "Mature" Region: The Re-making of Management–Labour Relations', unpublished paper, University of Sussex, 1984.
7. W. Brown, 'The Changing Role of Trade Unions in the Management of Labour', University of Warwick, paper given at conference, Queen Mary College, University of London, 1986.
8. MORI, *British Public Opinon*, Vol. VI, No. 8, September 1984; *EPIC Survey of Industrial Relations and Employee Communications*, Winter 1985.
9. Speech to IPM conference, Harrogate, 17 October 1985.
10. Acas briefing note to staff, 3/1984.
11. Speech to Fabian Society meeting, Blackpool, 3 September 1985.
12. 'Japanese Investments in Western Europe: a Jetro survey', London, 1983.
13. 'The State of Operation in Japanese Affiliates (Manufacturing) in Europe', London, 1985.
14. Speech to IPM conference, Harrogate, 25 October 1984.
15. *TUC Annual Report, 1985.*
16. *Ibid.*
17. W. Brown in *The Changing Contours of British Industrial Relations* (Oxford, 1981), puts the figure at 52 per cent, though he suggests that multi-unionism increases sharply as the size of the workforce grows. W. Daniel and N. Millward in *Workplace Industrial Relations in Britain*

(London, 1983), suggest it is 56 per cent. E. Batstone, *Working Order* (Oxford, 1985), places it much lower at 24 per cent, but his fieldwork concentrates on manufacturing industry, where multi-unionism is strongest.

18. *Works Management*, November 1985.
19. *Guardian*, 31 July 1985.
20. *TUC Annual Report, 1985.*
21. Morgan and Sayer, 'A "Modern" Industry in a "Mature" Region'.
22. Confidential TUC paper presented to employment policy committee, 17 December 1985.
23. Speech to IPM conference, Harrogate, 17 October 1985.
24. See Technical Change Centre, *Towards the Flexible Craftsman* (London, 1985).
25. E. Batstone, S. Gourlay, H. Levie and R. Moore, *Union Structure and Strategy in the Face of Technical Change*, (Oxford, 1986).
26. 'From Craftsman to Programmer', *AUEW Journal*, June 1984.
27. TUC paper to economic committee, 13 November 1985.
28. See, for instance, 'New Forms of Work Organisation', *IMS Manpower Commentary No. 30*, 1985.
29. See C. Dunkley, *Television Today and Tomorrow* (London, 1985).
30. NEDC paper, 21 November 1985.
31. Speech to IPM conference, Harrogate, 17 October 1985.
32. TCC, *Towards the Flexible Craftsman.*
33. TUC paper to economic committee, 13 November 1985.
34. *Financial Times*, 7 August 1985.
35. *Ibid.*, 24 July 1985.
36. Sir Ronald Edwards, *An Experiment in Industrial Relations* (Electricity Council, 1967).
37. Speech to IPM conference, Harrogate, 21 October 1983.
38. 'Developments in Harmonisation', *Acas Discussion Paper No. 1*, March 1982.
39. J. Dunning, *Japanese Participation in British Industry: Trojan Horse or Catalyst for Growth?* (London, 1986).
40. See, respectively: *Industrial Relations Review and Report*, No. 237, December 1980; speech to IPM conference, Harrogate, 18 October 1985; *Industrial Relations Review and Report*, No. 338, February 1985; *Financial Times*, 4 October 1985.
41. See J. Elliott, *Conflict or Co-operation* (London, 1978).
42. Speech to IPM conference, Harrogate, 26 October 1984.
43. 'General Principle of the CoAB System', Toshiba paper, March 1981.
44. *CAC Annual Report, 1984.*
45. Sir John Wood, 'Last Offer Arbitration', *British Journal of Industrial Relations*, Vol. XXIII, No. 3, November 1985.
46. *Acas Review of Arbitration Services*, 1981.
47. Department of Employment, 'Arbitration Arrangements in the Public Sector', paper prepared for Cabinet economic committee, November 1981.

48. *Ibid.*
49. Institute of Directors, *Settling Disputes Peacefully*, August 1984.
50. *Acas Review of Arbitration Services*, 1981.
51. See the *Journal of Conflict Resolution, passim.*
52. C. Stevens, 'Is Compulsory Arbitration Compatible with Bargaining?' *Industrial and Labor Relations Review*, 5, February 1966.
53. *Ibid.*
54. R. Hoh, 'The Effectiveness of Mediation in Public Sector Arbitration Systems: The Iowa Experience', *Arbitration Journal*, Vol. 39, No. 2, June 1984.
55. A. DeNisi and J. Dworkin, 'Final Offer Arbitration and the Naive Negotiator', *Industrial and Labor Relations Review*, Vol. 35, October 1981.
56. *Acas Annual Report, 1984.*
57. Acas briefing note to staff, 3/1984.
58. *Acas Annual Report, 1984.*
59. *CAC Annual Report, 1984.*
60. Wood, 'Last Offer Arbitration'.
61. 'Memorandum on No-strike Agreements in Public Services Other Than the Civil Service', Treasury memorandum of evidence to Megaw Committee, 1981.
62. Confidential TUC paper to employment committee, 18 July 1984.
63. *Ibid.*
64. 'Procedure Agreement Questionnaires', Acas internal paper, 1983.
65. 'Agreement on Trade Union Organisation in (Essential Intelligence Areas in) GCHQ', draft CCSU paper, 1984.

Chapter 7: Strike Free: The Testbed

1. EETPU press release, 2 April 1981.
2. *IDS Report*, various.

Chapter 8: Strike Free: The Deals Spread

1. *Hitachi and You*, Hitachi Consumer Products UK company members' handbook, 1985.
2. *Financial Times*, 27 January 1986.
3. 'New Future at Hirwaun', Hitachi internal document, April 1984.
4. See Acas briefing note to staff, 3/1984.
5. Figures supplied by unions concerned to TUC, apart from non-union figure, supplied by Hitachi, May 1984.
6. Internal TUC report of Hitachi disputes committee case, 16 January 1985.
7. Letter to Willis, 25 June 1985.
8. Letter to Webb, 6 August 1985.
9. Acas, briefing note to staff, 3/1984.
10. 'Weekend World', London Weekend Television, 29 January 1984.
11. Letter to the author, 26 March 1986.

12. Unpublished Acas report to Bowman Webber arbitration, by J. V. Davies, LLB.

Chapter 9: Strike Free: New Ways in Old Industries

1. D. Marsden, T. Morris, P. Willman and S. Wood, *The Car Industry: Labour Relations and Industrial Adjustment* (London, 1985).
2. *Financial Times*, 26 November 1985.
3. Speech to Industrial Relations Services conference, Brussels, 30 May 1985.
4. *Personnel Management*, August 1985.
5. 'File on Four', BBC, 28 January 1986.
6. *Daily Mail*, 15 May 1985.
7. Marsden *et al.*, *The Car Industry: Labour Relations and Industrial Adjustment*.
8. *Financial Times*, 20 January 1986.
9. *Works Management*, September 1985.
10. *Guardian*, 14 January 1986.
11. *Financial Times*, 4 January 1986.
12. See, for a full account of Shah, D. Goodhart and P. Wintour, *Eddie Shah and the Newspaper Revolution* (London, 1986).
13. Sogat '82, *New Technology – The American Experience* (London, 1985).

Chapter 10: The Alternative: No Unions, No Strikes

1. *IBM UK News*, 6 January 1986.
2. 'Information Technology, Employment and Entrepreneurship', paper to OECD conference, Paris, 18 November 1985.
3. *IBM UK News*, 6 January 1986.
4. Memorandum to House of Lords select committee on overseas trade, 1985.
5. *IBM Annual Review 1985*.
6. *IBM Employee Handbook*, September 1985.
7. *Acas, Report 44: IBM UK Ltd and ASTMS, AUEW (Engineering Section), AUEW–TASS, EETPU/EESA*, 4 July 1977.
8. *IBM Employee Handbook*.
9. Acas, *Report 44*.
10. 'Open Door', IBM internal publication.

Chapter 11: Strike Free: New Industrial Relations and the Future

1. 'File on Four', BBC, 28 January 1986.
2. W. Brown, 'The Changing Role of Trade Unions in the Management of Labour', University of Warwick, 1986.
3. Laird, on 'File on Four'.
4. *TUC Strategy*, 1984.

Index